DEDICATED TO A FUTURE OF AGRICULTURE

THAT NOURISHES OUR LAND, OUR COMMUNITY,

AND OUR FAMILIES. THIS IS FOR THE CHILDREN

OF ALL SPECIES, FOR ALL TIME.

COM-
MUNITY
TABLE

Recipes for an Ecological Food Future

THE ECOLOGY CENTER

pH **powerHouse Books**
Brooklyn, NY

COMMUNITY TABLE:
RECIPES FOR AN ECOLOGICAL FOOD FUTURE

Published in the United States by powerHouse Books, a division of powerHouse Cultural Entertainment, Inc.
32 Adams Street, Brooklyn, NY 11201-1021
e-mail: info@powerHouseBooks.com
website: www.powerHouseBooks.com

First edition, 2018

Library of Congress Control Number: 2018951667

ISBN 978-1-57687-882-8

10 9 8 7 6 5 4 3 2 1

Printed and bound in China through Asia Pacific Offset

CONTRIBUTORS

Executive Director, The Ecology Center
Evan Marks

Project Wrangler
Anna Maria Desipris

Writer
Lindsey Bro

Art Direction by
Nereo Zago
David Rager

Layout and Design
Kristi Day

Photographer
Aubrey Devin

Additional Photography
Scott Sporleder
Michelle Montgomery
Anne Watson
Ryan Haack
Mariusz Jeglinski
Taylor Allen Abeel

Recipe Editors
Amanda Yee
Kathryn Rogers

ACKNOWLEDGEMENTS

A special thank you to the long term supporters of The Ecology Center:

Anne Earhart, Beto and Tamar Bedolfe, Sara and Jack Lowell, Kelly and Jim Hallman, Jim and Sheila Peterson, Vicki and David Marks, Kristin Morrison, David Rager and Cheri Messerli, Alice Waters, Rick Bolton, Joe Baird, Caitlin Wege, Ann and Jim Shea, Mark Magiera, Ben Edwards, Laura Donovan, Jennifer Sherman, Eric Paine, Christie Mclean, Rita Howe, Kay Taygan.

Also, thank you to the Kickstarter backers who made this project possible:

Terry Otsuki, Amy Yeung, Barbara Helton, Nicole Smith, Susan Seely, Michael Stewart, Robyn Vettraino Jepsen, Linda and Marty Weiss, Lynda Ruth, Marlene Ruderman, Mim Michelove, Francoise Cuzor, Carla Malloy, Daniel Jackson, Jessica A. Gonzalez, Marty Enniss, Jaime Reed, Kay Sandland, Michael Besancon, Marina Goffredo, Julie Ellis, Jason McLeod, Joe Baird, Anne Dahlem, Michele Kato, Cathy McKnight, Heidi Kaspers, Robert Oesterreich, Jennifer Segerstrom, Audrey Boixo, Eric Paine, Evelyn Kodama, Sheila Peterson, Maureen Quigley, Kirk Vartan, Caitlin Wege, Alonzo Cudd, Tristan Prettyman Maris & Family, Leslie Weaver, Suz Schwartz, Cheryl Hammond, Verne Lusby, Monica Carter, Manuella Melchert, Eileen Kawas, Suzi, Ryan, Jeremy & Luiza Black

Printed on FSC® certified paper stock with soy-based inks.

FSC
www.fsc.org
MIX
Paper from responsible sources
FSC® C012521

Our vision is to build a **culinary community** that engages **consumers, farmers, chefs,** and **purveyors.**

Our purpose is to develop **a committed community of local chefs and restaurants** who incorporate **sustainable, best practices** into their businesses.

The Ecology Center acts as a hub for the **thoughtful dialogue** and collaboration that improves our food community.

The Ecology Center is a **valuable resource for sustainability**. Together, we create a network of purveyors and ecologically friendly products and brands, while also **educating our community about the tools** needed for efforts like recycling and composting.

CONTENTS

6   Foreword by Alice Waters

8   Introduction by Evan Marks

10   The Ecology Center

12   Community Table Accord

16   Green Feast with Alice Waters

10 PRINCIPLES
FOR AN ECOLOGICAL FOOD FUTURE

36   ## EAT FRESH + SEASONAL
Choose local produce that's in season.

42   Peter Schaner / Schaner Family Farms

46   Chef Kerri Cacciata / Our Table Cooperative

62   ## BUY LOCAL
Support a dynamic local economy.

68   Scott Breneman / The Dory Fleet Fish Market

72   Chef Paddy Glennon / Clausen Oysters

76   Chef Jason McLeod / Ironside Fish & Oyster

92   ## CHOOSE ORGANIC
Remove contaminants and toxins from our food supply.

98   George Kibby / South Coast Farms

102   Chefs Flemming Hansen & Mette Helbæk / Stedsans

118   ## RESPECT ANIMALS
Only eat animals raised with intention and respect.

124   Krystina Cook / Cook Pigs Ranch

128   Michael Puglisi / Electric City Butcher

132   Chef Ryan Adams / 370 Common

148   ## GROW YOUR OWN
Participate in the act of growing food.

154   Evan Marks / Marks Homestead

158   Megan Penn / Orange Home Grown

162   Chef Greg Daniels / Haven Gastropub

178 **CELEBRATE DIVERSITY**
Cultivate and consume a diverse variety of foods.

184 Makoto Chino / Chino Family Farms
188 Chefs Ryan & Nikki Wilson / Five Crowns

204 **PROMOTE POLYCULTURES**
Make farms regenerative ecosystems.

210 Alex Weiser / Weiser Family Farms
214 Anna Maria Desipris / Beekeeper
218 Chef Rich Mead / Farmhouse at Roger's Gardens

232 **NOURISH ALL CHILDREN**
Give all children access to delicious, healthy food.

238 Holly Carpenter / The Growing Experience
242 Chef Paul Buchanan / Primal Alchemy

256 **EDUCATE FOR CHANGE**
Empower positive change through personal and collective activism.

262 Mark Wagner / Palmquist Elementary School
266 Chef Jennifer Sherman / Chez Panisse

282 **CELEBRATE THE HARVEST**
Take time to celebrate, recognize, and inspire your community.

288 Nan Kohler / Grist & Toll
292 Louie & Clinton Prager / Prager Brothers Artisan Breads
296 Chef David Pratt / Brick

314 Recipes by Season
316 California Crops by Season

"Feeding one another, and offering children a healthy path to grow in body and spirit, is an act of the greatest love and respect for humanity. Caring for the land is an act of the greatest love and respect for the planet that nourishes us. Eating is an agricultural act and a political act, and a way to educate our senses. It can change the way we treat each other, and it can change the world."

Foreword

BY ALICE WATERS

"If we really want to fix the food system in this world, if we really want to make lasting change, then the greatest thing we can do is educate and empower the next generation. School is where we can reach all children while their habits are still being formed and their senses are marvelously alive and open. When they inevitable fall in love with real food, then they embrace the values that have brought that food to the table. This is why I believe so profoundly in edible education. It changes lives forever."

On my first visit to The Ecology Center in San Juan Capistrano, I knew instantly I had come to a very special place. Similar to our first Edible Schoolyard in Berkeley, what had started as an abandoned lot and some dirt had been transformed into a bountiful garden, teaching kitchen, and community center where people could come to connect around food, the environment, and the power of an edible education. I immediately fell in love with the space, and the people who created it.

Work that is transformative takes time and care. It also takes the right people in sometimes the most unexpected places – like southern Orange County – where Evan and his dedicated staff have built a resource for the people, families, and children living there. Their willingness to invest in the communities, schools, and educators who care about children's health and learning; promote healthy families and social connections; and support the sustainable farmers who are stewarding the land for generations to come, is an inspiration to me. They have not only joined our rapidly growing movement, they have created a thriving model with a simple truth at its core: food is what connects us to everything else in life.

This is the guiding principle for everything we do at Chez Panisse, the restaurant I opened nearly 50 years ago. Some people think it was a radical act, but I think it was just radically simple! To be perfectly honest, as many people already know, I only started the restaurant to have a place for my friends to come, and to eat the way I had eaten in France, where my senses had been awakened for the first time. But it did not take long for me to realize that there was so much more at stake. Most importantly, that how we approach food – the way we grow, purchase, and consume it – has a profound and lasting effect on agriculture, culture, the environment, and our health. In this way, eating is an ecological act, a belief we cook with every day at the restaurant, and one I am proud to share with The Ecology Center and countless others.

In writing this book, *Community Table*, The Ecology Center has produced yet another example of the kind of important and impactful work they do. Not because we need another cookbook – or even another restaurant for that matter – but because we need more good conversations, and more tables being set that reflect our values and beliefs. 🌱

"How we nourish the soil is how we nourish ourselves and how we nourish ourselves is how we view the world.

This isn't just another cookbook with beautiful recipes, this is a manual and a starting point."

Introduction

BY EVAN MARKS

The story of food is constant. It jumps borders, bridges gaps, and gives us the chance, rather honestly, to see our values for what they really are. And that's where this project started. It began with the question: *What if we were to literally bring people to the table to have a conversation about the future of food and our role in it?* Our solution became the Community Table Accord and its corresponding dinner series.

As 12 meals throughout the year – ten more-intimate, seasonally inspired, 50-person affairs book-ended by two, in the spring and autumn, 200-person celebrations – the dinners are a cornerstone of connection, bringing together the best chefs and most treasured farmers in, and beyond, our bioregion. Each dinner was themed around one of the ten principles we laid out as the path to an ecological food future; in turn, in turn, we paired a chef with a principle they were inspired by, tasking them with the goal of embodying that principle from seed to soup. This would include everything from sourcing, to technique, to their final menu.

There's something magical that happens when you get people around a table, engaged in meaningful conversation, breaking bread, connecting, and consciously looking for solutions to build an abundant future. It's progressive and challenging and so interesting that the mere act of sharing a good meal – one made with ingredients grown with integrity and purpose – can be a radical act.

Right now, our culture is at a critical tipping point and we can continue on the path we've laid, or we can collectively shift toward a future that's holistic, abundant, and connected.

The Ecology Center started nine years ago when we transformed into a place where community could gather together and have hands-on experiences around ecological solutions. One of the first things we did was put a long table out in the middle of the field, inviting 200 friends, strangers, and neighbors to begin the conversation around what a sustainable Southern California food community could look like.

The answer started in the form of "relationship." "Relationship" not only to ourselves and our communities, but to nature. The principles laid out here are designed to get us back in alignment with the innately regenerative nature of the world. It's about seeing our schools, backyards, agriculture and nourishment as nature, and in turn, ourselves.

These principles, and this book, are focused on the idea of getting to an ecological food future, but the reality is it's a never-ending journey. This is about the scaled, tangible solutions that can push us toward empowered dialogue and participation. We are conscious individuals and, truthfully, we have no idea how far our ripple can go – that's what's so exciting.

Community Table: Recipes for an Ecological Food Future specifically starts with the farmer first. At the end of the day, chefs and farmers are artists, universally valued for their craft, but chefs seem to get more of the spotlight. For us, it starts with the farmer because we can't do anything without good ingredients. 🌱

The Ecology Center

WE STRIVE FOR A CULTURE SHIFT ONE DAY AT A TIME

Watching a place transform inspires communities to take action. That's what we believe at The Ecology Center and, over the last nine years, we've transformed an unoccupied house and dirt lot into a beautiful, thriving community organization focused on shifting behavior.

The Ecology Center started as an experiment to see if we could transform a culture of cars, cul-de-sacs, and consumerism toward one of ecological thought. While most environmental organizations have approached the topic with negativity, we decided to come at it with solutions first. At The Ecology Center, we believe in the motivational power of possibility and hope. We create and model solutions for thriving on planet Earth.

We believe in a culture that gives more than it takes, one that learns from conversations and action. We design experiences that invite movement toward lasting emotional memories, believing that once you connect, you'll understand. We strongly believe in modeling authentic solutions that can be exported, scaled, and replicated. Together, we are catalysts for transformation and we believe in the power of showing up, seeing, touching, feeling, and participating in designing our future.

By providing knowledge-based tools and hands-on training for individuals, families, and communities, we've watched change spread. We hope this book is one step in the right direction for all of us and we hope you are inspired to join the journey, showing our children what a healthy future looks, tastes, and feels like.

"Our planet needs more examples of humanity working to support all living systems. We seek to be the best FOR the world, not the best in the world. We live it in our day-to-day across all aspects of our work – the demonstration that a positive future is possible."

Community Table Accord

WE BELIEVE IN
THE POWER OF ACTION

When we realized how desperate the state of our food system was, we knew the biggest thing we could do was to galvanize our resources. By bringing the community together, we could inspire acts of tangible change and then progress from there. After talking to chefs and farmers, we discovered what was really needed was a commitment and a resource. So we gathered our knowledge and put together a list.

The result is the Community Table Accord, a mainstreamed resource for sustainability in the global farm-to-table movement. The Accord and the 10 Principles that accompany it were shaped by our founding chefs and, together, we practice it.

> "Our food should nourish both people and place."

On a large scale, we have worked with chefs at our farm dinner for nearly a decade, on a smaller scale, we constantly work with chefs for small events, sourcing, and so many other things throughout the year. As a result, we've had countless conversations about what chefs actually need in their industry to start making sustainable shifts. We learned that they wanted to make local sourcing techniques, and the like, part of their day-to-day practices at their restaurants, but they needed to know how.

As we see it, chefs are leaders and teachers in their communities. They can be a powerful point of inspiration and change for those around them, so if they are asking for resources, we know they are just the starting point. That's why we created the Community Table Accord: so we could provide a quick, clear, concise framework for chefs to know what we're talking about when we talk about sustainability.

To shape the Accord, making sure it was useful and manageable, we gathered inspirational chefs from our region, all found in this book, to come together with Alice Waters, signing a commitment to be the leaders in their community of this mission. By launching the Community Table Accord, we set into motion a commitment to an aspirational, attainable, and delicious future.

We're all in this together. ❧

Green Feast
with Alice Waters

...AND 200 OF OUR CLOSEST FRIENDS

Since the first Green Feast nine years ago, we've gathered the best chefs in our region, invited our community, and hosted a celebration of truly ecological food.

Everything, from the salt to the olive oil, is sourced from within 250 miles of San Juan Capistrano, and it shows us just how truly delicious food can be.

In 2016, Green Feast was hosted by our hero, Alice Waters, bringing together a community of chefs, farmers, and friends to share a truly magical and unforgettable meal.

From the salt to the olive oil, every single ingredient for Green Feast has to be sourced from within 250 miles of San Juan Capistrano. This is the challenge our chefs face: how to create a beautiful meal that celebrates the season and the farmers, our community, and the work we've done.

This is the power of food: to bring people together, to shape a delicious future, and remind us of our responsibility for our part in it all.

Food is both an environmental and a social issue. It shows what our values are and what we deem important as a whole. We have to put value in our food, our farmers, and our sourcing. As consumers, if we don't let it be known that we care, a shift can't happen.

With a long table set for 200 on the farm, it's a magical setting for our chefs to work. Many of them choose to harvest herbs and various ingredients from the property, gathering table decorations and finishing garnishes alike. Right, Chef Jennifer Sherman forages fig leaves for plating. Above, last of the season's heirloom tomatoes are roasted and dressed simply with herbs.

Inspiration is part of our mission. Seeing what's possible is powerful.

At the end of the evening, chefs and volunteers gather to commemorate another beautiful meal. Discussion topics included the accessibility of organic food in schools, the importance of treasuring our farmers, and how we could take action beyond this table.

GAZPACHO
with lime, chili, & cilantro flowers

Serves 6

5	assorted very ripe, juicy varietal tomatoes
¼ cup	extra virgin olive oil, plus 2 Tbl
4	sprigs basil
-	kosher salt
2	cloves garlic, peeled and gently crushed
2 Tbl	sherry vinegar, or to taste
1	medium red onion
1	medium Mediterranean style cucumber
1	medium sweet red pepper
1	jalapeño
-	cilantro or basil flowers

Wash, drain, and cut tomatoes into chunks. Place in bowl with all seeds and juice, 1 teaspoon kosher salt, the garlic cloves, and basil sprigs. Chill for 4 hours, covered in refrigerator.

Remove garlic and basil and pass through a food mill, removing seeds and skins. Return tomato purée to refrigerator.

Make garnish: finely dice red onion and place in a bowl with 1 tablespoon of the sherry vinegar and ½ teaspoon salt. Chill. Finely dice cucumber, sweet pepper, and jalapeño and combine and chill in refrigerator. Can be made up to 8 hours ahead.

When ready to serve, whisk ¼ cup olive oil and remaining 1 tablespoon sherry vinegar into tomato soup base and taste for seasoning. Adjust as necessary, remembering that the garnish will be spicy and tangy with vinegar too. Combine marinated onions with cucumber mixture and remaining 2 tablespoons olive oil.

Ladle chilled tomato soup into chilled bowls and garnish with a large spoonful of the cucumber mixture. Sprinkle with cilantro or basil flowers or your fresh herbs of choice!

NEW GARLIC & GOAT CHEESE SOUFFLÉ

Serves 4

5 Tbl	butter, plus 2 Tbl
4 Tbl	AP flour
1 cup	whole milk
-	salt and black pepper
1 cup	green garlic or leek, sliced and washed
¼ cup	heavy cream
4	eggs
¼ cup	fresh goat cheese
2	sprigs fresh thyme, picked and chopped
2 Tbl	Italian parsley, chopped

In a small saucepan melt 5 tablespoons butter and add flour to make a roux. Cook over low heat for about 5 minutes, continuously stirring and scraping the roux off the bottom and sides of the pan. Remove pan from heat.

In a separate saucepan, heat milk to just below a simmer. Whisk milk into slightly cooled roux and cook, stirring for 5 minutes on low, until it becomes a creamy and smooth béchamel. Add salt and black pepper to taste and put aside to cool.

Melt remaining 2 tablespoons butter in a saucepan and add green garlic. Cook gently, adding a tablespoon of water if needed, until garlic is tender and mild. Blend with the cream in a blender until smooth and add to the béchamel.

Preheat oven to 375°F and butter an approximately 9x7-inch heavy glass or ceramic baking dish. Separate the egg yolks from the whites and reserve the whites in a bowl for whisking. Mix the yolks, goat cheese, thyme, and parsley into the béchamel mixture. Add a pinch of salt to the whites and whisk to stiff but not dry peaks. Fold into mixture. Spoon mixture into baking dish and bake for 25-30 minutes or until the soufflé is fully puffed. Bring to the table and serve immediately!

GREEN BEAN, CORN, & SHELL BEAN RAGOUT

Serves 4

½ lb	best quality in season green beans (or Romano beans or yellow wax beans)
3 cups	fresh shelled beans (cannellini, flageolet, cranberry, etc)
¼ cup	olive oil, plus 1 Tbl
1	bay leaf
-	salt and pepper
1	yellow onion, diced
2	cloves garlic, pounded and covered with 1 Tbl olive oil
2 ears	sweet corn, shucked and kernels cut off
2	sprigs fresh savory or thyme or basil, roughly chopped

Top and tail green beans. Cook quickly in a pot of salted boiling water until just tender. Let cool spread out on a baking sheet and reserve.

Place shelled beans in a pot just covered by an inch with water. Add 1 tablespoon olive oil, the bay leaf, and 1 teaspoon of salt. Let simmer until beans are tender, adding more water if necessary to keep the beans just covered. Let the beans cool in their liquid, drain, and reserve, saving ½ cup of the bean cooking water.

In a large sauté pan, add the olive oil and onions and cook until the onions are tender. Add salt and pepper, the crushed garlic, and the corn. Cook gently for 5 minutes until the corn is just barely cooked.

Finally add the shelled beans, their liquid, and the green beans. Continue cooking until the flavors have come together. Add the herbs just before serving. Adjust for salt, pepper, or a dash more of good olive oil. Serve immediately.

SALMON GRILLED IN FIG LEAF

Serves 4

4 ea	4 oz salmon fillets, boneless and skinless
4 Tbl	olive oil
-	salt and pepper
4	Meyer lemon wedges
4	young, fresh fig leaves, approximately 8" diameter

Preheat oven to 400°F or start wood fire or charcoal grill. Sprinkle the salmon fillets with salt and pepper to taste. Brush the fig leaves (top side up) with olive oil and coat the fillets with the remainder.

Place the fillets on the leaves, wrap the leaves over loosely, and place in a baking dish or baking sheet. Bake in the oven approximately 15 minutes or until the fillets feel slightly firm. If grilling, start on folded side of leaf and grill approximately 3 minutes on each side.

Place packets on warm plates and open leaf slightly. Garnish with a lemon wedge and another drizzle of olive oil if you wish.

STUFFED APRICOTS

Serves 4

6-8	medium size apricots of local variety, we love Blenheim or Patterson
¼ cup	whole almonds
4	amaretti cookies
3 Tbl	salted butter
2 tsp	sugar, plus more for dusting
1	small egg yolk
-	pinch of flour
1 tsp	brandy

Toast almonds in 350°F oven until lightly toasted. Chop almonds and amaretti in a food processor until just ground.

Beat butter and sugar until fluffy, add yolk and continue beating. Add in flour and crushed cookie/almond mixture and dash of brandy to taste.

Cut apricots in half and remove pit. Place in a heavy baking dish and place a small scoop of the filling in each apricot. Sprinkle lightly with sugar.

Bake in a 375°F oven for about 15 minutes or until the filling puffs and the fruit begins to soften. Serve while still slightly warm with vanilla ice cream or vanilla parfait.

CHOOSE LOCAL PRODUCE
THAT'S IN SEASON

Eat Fresh
+ Seasonal

Certain foods grow at certain times for a reason. Based on varying climates and seasons, different varietals will be available and it's important to begin by eating what's in season. In doing so, you reduce your use of resources, you consume better food, and you directly support a dynamic local economy.

Eat Fresh + Seasonal

THE FIRST STEP IS TO GET BACK IN ALIGNMENT WITH NATURE.

Seasons naturally flow in and out of one another, connecting what one needs to what the others can provide. We believe that living in rhythm with these natural patterns means living in abundance.

In real life, eating seasonally and eating fresh is really about following what nature provides. Since weather and region dictate what we grow, different seasons offer different things. Summer has tomatoes, pickles, peppers, peaches, figs, berries, and fruit; and if we can learn a few simple preservation skills, we can then enjoy the bounty of summer in the depths of winter.

Currently, our conventional model for acquiring food lacks connection. Where we purchase produce is more about packaged convenience than seasonality or nutrition. Have you ever wondered why you're buying food next to toiletries and cleaning supplies? Hopefully, in the future, we'll purchase produce and dry goods separately, investing in small businesses throughout our local community, but until then, we have to find points of purchase that reflect the seasons.

"In spring, we should expect to see spring greens, and in summer we should look forward to stone fruits; autumn should be full of anticipation for gourds, and winter should be hearty with root vegetables."

Part of eating fresh and seasonal is also preparing for what comes next. During summer we make a practice of saving seeds for the following year, processing the abundance of one season so we can enjoy it again. Another thing is our attitude toward seasonal food. It's easy to miss certain fruits and vegetables when they aren't growing, but part of the experience of seasonal eating is to find joy in the anticipation of planting garlic, potatoes, lettuce, carrots, and beets. Seasonality is about surrendering to the ebb and flow.

Eating fresh and seasonal is also a matter of efficiency: it takes less energy to produce and consume food that is fresh, local, and in season. Though it all

blurs together, eating what's in season is also about eating the best quality food, and this usually shows up by growing your own produce. Beyond the economy of a fresh and seasonal diet, homegrown food is more delicious, has higher nutrition, and benefits the local economy in unparalleled ways. Add its ability to build community, support the environment, and discover a sense of self-sufficiency, and we realize how integral seasonal eating is to an ecological lifestyle.

> "Seasonal food is about discovering self-sufficiency, exploring creativity, cooking, and enjoying the abundance of variety."

Something we all have to recognize is that we can no longer take food for granted. We have to know where it comes from and what time of year we should be getting it. Traveling to the tropics, fresh fruit is everywhere and when we're there, we should eat a lot of bananas, but

we should not eat them in the middle of a city where banana trees don't grow.

Over the years, our economy of convenience has created an expectation for the most common foods to be available whenever and wherever we want. Our challenge is to ask ourselves what that convenience is worth. When food has to travel a long distance to get to you, that means a lot of resources have been used to transport it and a lot of energy has been used to keep it fresh; moreover, it likely did not fully mature before being picked and it probably has not only less flavor, but also less nutrition than something grown locally.

You have to commit to truly eating in season. It's a delicious dedication, but it's still dedication at the end of the day. At The Ecology Center, we've made a promise to not eat food grown outside of our bioregion or outside of its season. We find it empowering to choose to eat local, to flow with the seasons, and to watch our diets shift as the season does.

Of course we get a little tired of tomatoes in late summer, but we can them so we can enjoy beautiful heirloom tomato sauce all year round. When we get tired of kale and chard, we realize they're going out of season soon enough and something else will step in to take their place.

Eating fresh and seasonal should be easy. By purchasing produce from small farmers who grow food without pesticides and toxins, you're supporting your local ecosystem. By also choosing to support farmers who grow foods in season for their bioregion, systematically growing a variety of crops from season to season, you're truly supporting the web it takes to keep our foodshed strong.

"Seasonality breeds diversity and diversity is key to a healthy body, a healthy community, and a thriving ecosystem."

Eating Fresh + Seasonal is really the *how* to how we're going to build a healthy food economy when we aren't all farmers, we aren't all cooks, and we aren't all fully engaged in a life dedicated to sustainability. That means your first step, and ours, is calibrating to the seasons. There's a time and place for everything, so take the time to find out what grows when in your region. The power of knowledge when you're out shopping or eating can be truly impactful. 🌱

When the weather changes, so should your plate.

HOME

Start by buying half your produce from the local farmers market

Plan weekly meals around seasonal fruits and vegetables

Phase out packaged and processed foods

RESTAURANT

Source all salad greens and at least one vegetable from the farmers market

Create a part of your menu that changes seasonally (i.e. salads and appetizers)

Educate your staff and customers on the importance of seasonality

Peter Schaner

Located about 25 miles east of the Pacific Ocean in northern San Diego County, Schaner Farms is a family-run operation on approximately 35 acres.

With about 90 varieties of fruit trees, the Schaners had to think creatively about how to maximize their soil. To do this, they've been using bottomland below their trees to grow vegetables and raise turkeys, duck, chicken, and guinea hens.

Since 1984, Peter and Kayne Schaner have raised their eight kids while farming seasonally. They practice rotation farming, selling direct to chefs and top restaurants throughout Southern California. Though they are not certified organic, they farm without pesticides or toxins, raising free-range birds on a diet of grain from a mill in Riverside, barley mash leftovers from local breweries, vegetables not sold at market, and leftover rinds and pulp from their juicing operation. In addition, they keep goats for milk, turkey, steer, and pigs for meat, and chickens for eggs.

Dedicated to their routine, they plant, weed, cultivate, and prune on Mondays, prepare for market on Tuesdays, sell on Wednesdays, farm on Thursdays, prepare for market on Fridays, and sell again on Saturdays.

IN CONVERSATION WITH THE SCHANER FAMILY

Farming for us is a family thing. I've followed in my dad's footsteps, and my older brother helps to organize the CSA program. My younger brothers are planning to come back and help on the farm, too; everyone tends to be involved during the summer, but I think it'll start to be a more year-round thing for all of us. Back in the day, my grandpa had a chicken ranch and my dad's grandparents had a farm. I guess it's in our blood.

It's fun working closely with chefs and the community because they create demand for us. We also educate them. For example, when avocados are done,

"When you grow for direct-to-consumer as opposed to the packing house, you actually see the people who benefit from your work. Both parties appreciate and support each other. You see the full circle. It's a complete relationship."

pomegranates are on their way in, so we try to make sure chefs know what to expect. That way they want what we're already going to have. It's really fun to work with chefs who actually want to constantly change their menu based on what you have, not just what they think the customer will want.

When something's out of season where you live, do you really want to eat something that lived in a shipping container for a few weeks?

Local produce costs a little more because water costs more here, but we've learned how to deal with the drought by watering differently. On our land, we have a few different kinds of sprayers, we use more drip tape, and we've focused a lot on how to utilize our well. Since the main thing we grow is citrus, it's been important to really figure out the amount of water citrus needs to make it through the drought. Our production has definitely gone down, but our quality is still there. We've also started picking different varieties of common things, for example avocado trees that have a different root system and use less water.

Part of the future of farming is about getting a younger generation interested in supporting farms. It's about education on where your food comes from and realizing it's not so much going out of your way to get food, it's just getting food.

As long as we have water, I think our future is positive.

"Part of the future of farming is about getting a younger generation interested in supporting farms. It's about education on where your food comes from and realizing it's not so much going out of your way to get food, it's just getting food."

"The key to a seasonal farm is having variety. You grow one thing and once that season is done, you're ready to replace it with two other things."

Kerri Cacciata

OUR TABLE COOPERATIVE;
SHERWOOD, OREGON

Inspired by clean, simple, and intricately spiced foods, Chef Kerri Cacciata is as dedicated to her ingredients as she is to their story. Interested in the politics of sourcing and seasonality, Chef Kerri's meal explored the importance of pollinators in an ecosystem and how intimately everything depends on them.

Having worked as a private chef for years, when Kerri joined The Ecology Center as their Chef in Residence, prior to moving to a cooperative farm in Oregon, she not only took on the responsibility of community education through food, but also the Community Table Accord. Through the Accord, Chef Kerri has helped to align the center's mission with the practicalities of a working kitchen and the needs of the chef. Together, they're shifting the way restaurants approach sourcing and seasonality.

"Alice Waters is a huge influence. Her story resonates with me and I want to bridge that gap between food and community."

IN CONVERSATION WITH CHEF KERRI CACCIATA

I grew up sort of fending for myself with food and it resulted in some serious health problems. At 11, my cholesterol was so high they had to place me on a vegan diet. That's when I learned about the link between food and health.

Today, I eat as much for health as I do for taste and emotion. It's funny because growing up my parents ran restaurants and I was always around food. Early on, I thought I wanted out of the industry, but when I was in San Francisco, I learned about Alice Waters and how she uses food as a tool to create community and it made so much sense. Suddenly, I didn't have to run quite so far from what I'd known and it was really easy to decide on culinary school.

The link, for me, is gardening. It was the key to how I got into food craft and the art of stocking a pantry. It started as this fascination around how to do essential things with integrity. So, I started taking classes at The Ecology Center, learning

"My diet and my menus really revolve around what I can get there, supplementing only the little things that are missing. My menu was veg heavy because of this, but what's wrong with that? I love flipping people's approach to meat on their plate."

about seed saving and the potential each season carries in the fruit of its labor. I think I saved a few heirloom varietals that first time and I've done it ever since.

I think for a lot of chefs who came up around the same time as me, Alice Waters was one of our first influences. After her, I read a lot of MFK Fisher. Falling in love with the romance to food and her voice gave my approach a tone I still resonate with today.

Because I'm not the most technique-driven person, I like to approach my work starting from the garden or farm, deciding everything else from there. That devotion to the ingredient, and using food to really say something, is absolutely inspired by Alice and MFK Fisher.

For me, actually living this way is life changing. Eating fresh and seasonal cuts out so many of the foods that are averse to our health. In turn, if you're eating seasonal, hopefully you're also sourcing locally, which in turn benefits the local food economy. As a result, seasonal eating can truly give our farmers a sense of job security that not much else can. From there, these farmers are able to then explore their craft in a more meaningful way. It's a food ecosystem.

It's amazing where food's at right now because farmers markets are every-where. You can do a quick search and likely find at least one market near you, and the farmers are all so interested in connecting. They want to answer questions and to tell you how to prepare the food. It's really such a fun resource. I try so many new things because of the purveyors, and it makes my food far more interesting. I almost always recommend shopping small for dry goods and sundries, too. Going bulk. Looking into a food co-op. Just exploring different options rather than the conventional route. ❧

"Relationships are everything. People are the best resource we have for passing on knowledge, education, skills...and we have to actively work to keep it alive."

"If sourcing with intention makes you just a little more thoughtful when you're plating, I think it's worth it."

MONTH

April

CHEF

Kerri Cacciata, Our Table Cooperative

FARM

Schaner Family Farms

At the height of spring, with foraged flowers and tender greens, Chef Kerri gathered an all-female crew to run her kitchen. Driven by the concept of diversity and its integral importance, Chef Kerri crafted a beautiful vegetarian menu, heavily emphasized by clean spices, eggs, and ingredient-focused execution.

Schaner Family Farms has nearly every type of egg-laying fowl on their property so it was no wonder eggs were everywhere in this dinner.

"Bringing together a group of women for this dinner was so important. There was such an energy of comradery and care, plus, they're all so talented. There's nothing as fun as cooking with your friends – well maybe cooking for your friends – but we got to do both."

– KERRI CACCIATA

TO START

Chilled baby veg with herbed butter

Medjool dates with rosewater, rosemary, and sea salt

MAINS

Tartine of burrata and first of the season cherries

Baby greens and spring vegetables with green goddess, falafel croutons, and fried quail egg

Pancotto: traditional bread soup with heirloom beans and grains, herb oil, and a slow poached guinea egg

Goat milk Greek yogurt gnocchi with coconut-curried root veg, blood orange, and cilantro

DESSERT

Ginger olive oil cake, salted vanilla cream, strawberries, rhubarb, lavender honey, seeds, and petals

CHILLED BABY VEG WITH HERBED BUTTER

Serves: 2-4

2 lbs   mixed baby vegetables
¼ cup   unsalted butter
3 Tbl   mixed fresh herbs, minced
1   lemon, zest only
-   salt and pepper

Bring butter to room temperature by leaving it out and covered for about 2-3 hours or until it becomes desired texture.

In a large bowl, clean vegetables, leaving a bit of the greens attached. Once clean, cut in half then place the vegetables on a parchment-lined sheet tray and set aside. In a small bowl, mix together room temperature butter, minced herbs and lemon zest using a rubber spatula until well combined. Salt and pepper to taste.

Holding each vegetable by the stem end, roll in butter mixture until fully coated. If needed, stir to soften further for even coating. Place each coated vegetable back onto the sheet tray, and when all are coated, place in refrigerator to set for 15-20 minutes. Serve cold.

Note: Use your favorite combination of herbs and citrus for the butter. If needed, you can substitute crudités for the baby vegetables.

MEDJOOL DATES

with rosewater, rosemary, and sea salt

Serves: 2-4

1 cup	Medjool dates, pitted
2 Tbl	rosewater
1	pinch of flaky sea salt
2	small sprigs rosemary, stems removed

Heat a medium pan over medium heat. Once pan is hot, add dates, rosewater, and rosemary. Stir until warmed through, dates are coated, and rosewater is absorbed, about 5-7 minutes.

Remove from heat, sprinkle sea salt over the top, and plate. Serve warm.

TARTINE OF BURRATA

with first of the season cherries

Serves: 2-4

2ft	crusty baguette
4 Tbl	extra virgin olive oil
1 lb	cherries, pitted
¼ cup	balsamic vinegar
8 oz	burrata, halved
-	sea salt and freshly ground pepper
-	microgreens and edible flowers, for decoration

Preheat oven to 350°F. While oven is heating, cut the baguette into ¼ inch slices, on a bias, so they are long and thin. Drizzle with oil olive and place directly on baking rack of oven until lightly toasted, but not crispy, about 5 minutes. Set aside.

In a non-reactive medium bowl, toss cherries with balsamic vinegar, and place onto a lined sheet tray. Roast in oven until cherries are softened and balsamic is sticky, about 15-18 minutes. Set aside.

Spread halved burrata on medium serving platter. Spread remaining burrata half on toasts, then top each with a spoonful of cherry and balsamic mixture and place on platter. Top with microgreens and edible flowers. Sprinkle with salt and pepper to taste.

PANCOTTO: BREAD SOUP

with heirloom beans and grains, herb oil, and slow-poached guinea egg

Serves: 4-6

6 cups	vegetable broth
2 Tbl	olive oil
3 cups	rustic crusty bread, preferably sourdough, cubed
1	large onion, diced
2	stalks of celery, diced
2	medium carrots, diced
½ cup	dried heirloom beans of choice
½ cup	wheat berries
3	medium tomatoes, chopped
½ cup	kale, chopped
5	garlic cloves, minced
1 Tbl	dried thyme
1 Tbl	dried oregano
1 tsp	crushed red pepper flakes
2 Tbl	lemon juice

TO GARNISH:

½ cup	Parmesan cheese
-	salt and pepper
-	herb oil (see note)
-	fresh herbs
1	guinea egg per bowl of soup

Heat large pot over medium heat. Once pot is hot, add oil, onion, celery, and carrot. Sauté until tender, about 5-7 minutes. Without stirring, turn heat to high, and allow vegetables to caramelize.

When color develops on mirepoix, deglaze pot with the vegetable broth and then lower heat to medium-low.

Add the wheat berries, beans, tomatoes, kale, and red pepper flakes to the pot and cook on medium-low for about 3-4 hours or until tender. Once soup is tender, add lemon juice and season with salt and pepper to taste.

10 minutes before serving, poach one egg for each bowl of soup. When plating, gently add the egg to the soup, then garnish with cheese, fresh herbs, and herb oil.

MAKING FLAVORED OILS: Start with a light tasting olive oil, and put into a pot with fresh herbs of your choice, garlic, a pinch of salt, and crushed red pepper. Gently simmer for 15-20 minutes. Do not boil. Boiling will affect the taste, losing the nuances and clean flavor of the oil and herbs. When cooled, store in fridge for up to a month.

FALAFEL CROUTONS AND QUAIL EGGS

on baby greens and spring vegetables with green goddess dressing

Serves: 2-4

1 lb	(about 2 cups) dry garbanzo beans
1	small onion, chopped
¼ cup	fresh parsley, chopped
3-5	cloves garlic
1½ Tbl	flour or chickpea flour
1¾ tsp	salt
2 tsp	cumin
1 tsp	ground coriander
¼ tsp	black pepper
¼ tsp	cayenne pepper
-	pinch of ground cardamom
12	quail eggs
1 Tbl	of butter, heaping
-	baby greens and vegetables

Soak beans fully submerged in water, overnight, about 12-24 hours. Once beans have bulked in size, drain and rinse.

In a food processor, combine all ingredients except eggs, butter, baby greens, and vegetables, and pulse until batter combines and looks like wet sand. Allow to sit for an hour at room temperature.

Heat oven to 375°F. Spread mixture on a baking sheet and bake for 15-25 minutes, or until golden brown and solid. Set aside.

10-15 minutes before serving, heat a medium pan on medium heat. Once hot, reduce to medium-low and add a generous spoonful of butter. Gently crack eggs over pan a few at a time and allow to fry until sunny side up, 2-5 minutes.

TO PLATE: In a medium bowl, toss vegetables with green goddess dressing (*see facing page*) until well coated. Place veggies on the bottom of a medium serving platter. Intersperse quail eggs on top of veggies, sprinkle croutons over salad and serve.

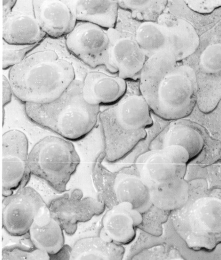

GREEN GODDESS DRESSING

Serves: 2-4

1	full cup of soft herbs like dill, cilantro, parsley, chives, and fennel frond, roughly chopped
1 Tbl	tahini
1 tsp	yellow mustard
⅓ cup	apple cider vinegar
1	clove garlic
1	shallot, minced
1 cup	olive oil
-	salt and pepper

Combine all ingredients except oil in a blender, and process until smooth. With blender on low, slowly stream in the oil until dressing is emulsified. Season with salt and pepper to taste.

Stores well in a mason jar in the refrigerator for up to 2 weeks.

NOTE: This is one of my favorite dressings, and it is very flexible based on what herbs you harvest or have on hand. Great as a dressing but also as a dip for crudités.

CURRIED ROOT VEGETABLES

Serves: 6-8

1 tsp	cumin seeds
1 tsp	fennel seeds
1 tsp	ground coriander
1 tsp	yellow mustard seeds
1 tsp	turmeric
1 tsp	curry powder
-	pinch of cinnamon
2 Tbl	coconut oil, warmed up to liquid state
3 lbs	choice of root vegetables like carrots, parsnips, beets, and celeriac
1 tsp	salt
½ tsp	black pepper

Preheat oven to 375°F.

Toast first six ingredients in a pan over medium until fragrant, about 3-5 minutes and set aside.

Cut vegetables into 1-inch pieces, drizzle with coconut oil and toss in a bowl with spices until coated. Spread onto a sheet tray and roast until tender and golden, about 20-25 minutes.

GOAT MILK / GREEK YOGURT GNOCCHI

with coconut curried root vegetables, blood orange, and cilantro

If you can't find goat yogurt, Greek yogurt would be the best substitution and is my go-to choice for gnocchi making.

Serves: 4-6

3 lbs	russet potatoes, washed
¾ cup	all purpose flour
2 Tbl	goat yogurt (if using Greek, full fat recommended over nonfat)
1	large egg yolk
1 Tbl	Parmesan cheese, finely grated on microplane
1 tsp	garlic powder
1 tsp	onion powder
1 tsp	sea salt
½ tsp	white pepper (black will also work in place of white)
1 Tbl	coconut oil

5-6	medium blood oranges (or 1 cup juice)

GNOCCHI: Bring oven to 425°F. Place potatoes on a sheet tray in a bed of kosher salt one inch deep and place in oven. After 20 minutes, rotate potatoes 180° in salt. Continue to bake until fully cooked through, about 40-50 minutes.

On a cutting board, cut potatoes in half lengthwise. Directly on your work surface and while potatoes are still hot, scoop the flesh out and put through a potato ricer (wearing gloves). Spread the riced potato out a bit for it to cool slightly. Set aside.

In a medium bowl, combine the yolk, yogurt, and spices, and drizzle evenly over the potatoes. Next, add an even layer of cheese on top of the potatoes. Then dust with ½ cup of the flour using a sieve or sifter. With a bench scraper, gently begin to fold the mixture onto itself a number of times until it comes together. With your hands, lightly pat into a loose dough ball. If it is very tacky, add the remaining flour and gently repeat without overworking the dough but until thoroughly combined. Dough should be moist but not sticky.

Scrape your work station, and dust with flour. Divide your dough into 4 sections, and begin to roll into ½ inch-thin logs using the palms of your hand. Dust with flour as needed. With the bench scraper, cut into 1-inch sized pieces, gently roll down the back of a gnocchi board or fork and set aside.

Heat a pan over medium flame, and once hot, add coconut oil. Add gnocchi 5-10 pieces at a time, making sure not to overcrowd the pan. Sear one side of the gnocchi until there is a golden color and a crisp texture. Pull from pan and set aside.

Best served hot, so have the vegetables and blood orange glaze ready to go.

BLOOD ORANGE REDUCTION: If you are lucky enough to find blood oranges in season, juice about 1 cup worth. If not, most fine markets offer blood orange juice in the refrigerated section. In a small pot, simmer on low heat for 30-40 minutes until reduced to about 50%.

TO PLATE: Place gnocchi and roasted vegetables on the plate, drizzle with blood orange reduction and sprinkle with fresh cilantro. Enjoy!

GINGER OLIVE OIL CAKE
with salted vanilla cream, strawberries, rhubarb, lavender honey, seeds, and petals

Serves: 4-6

3	large eggs
1 cup	cane sugar
⅔ cup	yogurt
1 Tbl	fresh ginger, grated fine
1¾ cup	unbleached AP flour
1½ cup	baking powder
¼ tsp	baking soda
¼ tsp	sea salt
⅔ cup	extra virgin olive oil, light in taste
-	butter or other oil for greasing

2	baskets of fresh strawberries, hulled
2	ribs of rhubarb, washed and sliced into ½ inch pieces
1 Tbl	honey

1 cup	organic heavy cream
1	vanilla bean
½ tsp	salt
2 tsp	honey

2-3 oz	honey
1 Tbl	lavender flowers

CAKE: Preheat your oven to 350°F. Combine eggs and sugar in the mixer (or a medium size bowl) with whisk attachment. Cream together for about 30 seconds, then add the yogurt and whisk again for one minute.

In a separate bowl, whisk together the next five ingredients.

Slowly combine the dry ingredients into the wet and then, on the lowest speed setting, drizzle in olive oil.

Pour into a greased, 9-inch springform pan (I prefer to use butter) and even out with a spatula.

Bake the cake until golden, about 50-55 minutes. Use a toothpick to test if the cake is done by pulling it in and out of the center of the cake. If the toothpick comes out clean, the cake is ready. Allow to cool for about one hour on a rack, and run a knife along the sides before unlatching pan.

STRAWBERRIES & RHUBARB: Preheat your oven to 375°F. Combine strawberries and rhubarb with one tablespoon honey in a bowl, mix, then spread out mixture on a lined sheet tray. Bake for about 12-15 minutes or until rhubarb is fork tinder. Set aside.

SALTED VANILLA CREAM: Combine 1 cup heavy cream, ½ teaspoon salt, 2 teaspoons honey and seeds of vanilla bean (cut vanilla bean in half and scrape seeds from the pod) and whisk until lightly whipped into soft peaks. Refrigerate until use.

LAVENDER HONEY GLAZE: In the tiniest pot on very low heat, warm honey with lavender in it for 20-25 minutes, making sure to not allow it to bubble or burn. Strain warm honey through a fine sieve to separate out lavender flowers.

TO PLATE: Plate a slice of the cake, top with fruit, then cream, and finally drizzle with a little of the honey. Garnish options: edible flower petals, and my favorite mix of seeds – chia, flax, and hemp.

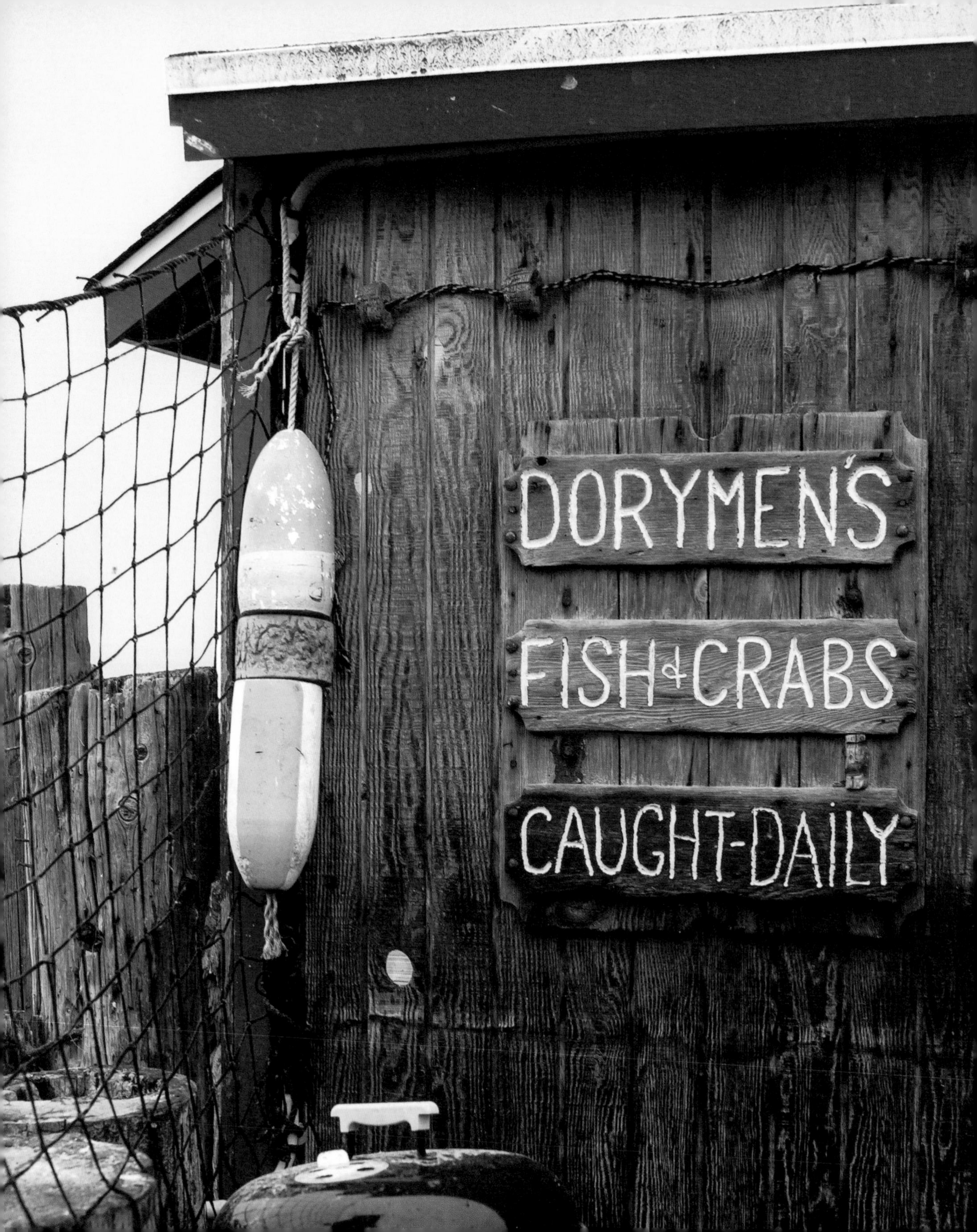

DORYMEN'S

FISH & CRABS

CAUGHT-DAILY

SUPPORT A DYNAMIC
LOCAL ECONOMY

Buy
Local

A vibrant local economy doesn't build
itself. It takes time, it takes community
and it takes purposeful support.
Fortunately, it's delicious.

Buy Local

THERE'S A STORY TO YOUR FOOD. GET TO KNOW IT.

Our foodsheds are full of food artisans who are passionate, full of integrity, and right in our own backyard.

Where you spend your money says what you support, so if you buy processed food, grown by big agriculture, you're feeding the conventional machine of nameless, faceless, and story-less food.

Instead, what if we were to put meaningful dollars in the hands of the people working to make our communities incredibly alive? What if we were to choose farmers, artisans, brewers, mead makers, cheese makers, grain growers, and bread makers from within our community? We want you to vote with your dollar by choosing to support local people, local systems, and progressive ideologies.

> "There's a growing consciousness around sourcing local. By buying local, you naturally eat with the seasons."

As a stepping stone from "Eat Fresh and Seasonal," "Buy Local" is about building local economy in all of our food systems, and we have the power to do that by being selective about what we purchase. "Eat Fresh and Seasonal" connects us to the seasons, our farmers markets, and hopefully starts to get people in the garden, getting their hands dirty. From there, "Buy Local" goes beyond just fruits and vegetables, taking us into the realm of food artisans. In our communities, foodsheds, and bio-regions, in order to really be sustainable, we have to rely on the people in our community to make the products we need.

By buying local, we are able to cultivate a collective process that stewards our landscape with a far deeper and wider reach than just produce. It keeps money in our community and it gives jobs to the people we live next door to. By purchasing value-added products grown and made with integrity, like local pickles, jams, and breads, we're supporting not only the energy it takes to grow it, but also the people passionate about the same things we're passionate about.

> "It's easy to buy local when local products are almost always the most delicious. They're made with the kind of integrity you can actually taste."

Really, the thing we're trying to avoid by buying local is buying things that are industrially processed. Usually, a product has traveled far – from out of the country or out of season – and it has likely been grown and transported in such a way that the practices and methods used are not in alignment with a sustainable, conscious, and regenerative food ecosystem. As a result, you are buying food without much love in it. And what does that really have to offer our vibrant food community in the future?

Practically speaking, what are the things that we can't produce in a "Buy Local" economy? Truly, not much. Over time, you will likely find a few things you cannot buy, but chances are that a lot of those things are not that important for daily consumption. Wine, for example: we have winemakers throughout Southern California who are doing an amazing job as stewards of agriculture, offering beautiful artisan products on the market. Because of the work they do, we do not think you have to import a lot of French wine for daily consumption. That does not mean that French wine is not amazing, but it allows for French wine to be special. It gives us the chance to really enjoy French wine on a daily basis when we go there. It lets us understand why French winemakers are incredibly talented at what they do and why they have done it in such a special way for so long. That is our thought, and we might be biased considering how much we love California and Californian wines, but cheese is the same thing. We live in a place without pasture so we have to expand

"If I can't get local fish, I don't eat fish, even if I want it."

– KERRI CACCIATA

"We are a reflection of nature. How we choose to sustain our food is a mirror of our ethics and our commitment to the landscape."

"US-caught wild fish guarantees not only the health of our local fisheries, but healthy conditions for everyone involved."

our local economy, or at least the reality of our local economy, when it comes to certain products like cheese. For Southern California, we have to look to Northern California to see what cheese makers from that region can fill our needs.

We do believe in buying local whenever possible because supporting local artisans directly benefits your community, but we do understand that you cannot get everything, always. Take the time to find the artisans that create products with integrity and intention, then fill in the gaps with other resources available to you.

A rich tradition of food artisans and methods of preservation have taught us that everything you can buy in the store can, in some way or another, come from our backyards and from local farmers. We challenge you to think beyond just the common stuff and to make a point to purchase things like fish from your local fish market, to be dedicated to doing your part to adding to the dynamic vibrancy of your local community.

At the end of the day, the people growing food, making products, and sustaining us need us to support them with our dollars, our commitment, and our connection. 🌱

Build a vibrant community. Buy local and demand products with a story of integrity.

HOME

Help turn your neighborhood into an *agrihood* (a community with gardens, collective dinners, and more)

When choosing seafood, focus on local sources and create meals around what's available

Sign up for a local CSA delivery (this can include a Community Supported Pantry subscription, an artisan food subscription, an Agricultural Apiary, and the like)

RESTAURANT

Ask for local produce from your distributor

Source from food artisans, supporting variety and regional differences

Build relationships with local farmers, fishermen, and producers at the market, naming them on your menu

Scott Breneman

As a fourth generation fisherman, Scott Breneman's family has fished with the Dory Fleet since the 1800s and early 1900s, but recently it's been just him and his father. After college, he got his own boat and took over the family permits that had been mostly unused since the decline of the fish docks in the 70s and 80s.

Over the years, he found himself dedicated to the principles of sustainable and regulated fishing; eventually building up a business, selling directly to local restaurants, and captaining three local boats in the process.

IN CONVERSATION WITH SCOTT BRENEMAN

Permits vary from species to species and for every species you catch, you have to have a separate permit. There are a limited number of permits, so the way it works is that you have to buy an existing permit from somebody else. The price range varies depending on how desperate the person is to sell it. There's not really a set market for it. A crab permit can go for as cheap as $25,000-$30,000 and a spot prawn permit can go for as much as almost a million dollars, so it depends on what you're going to catch.

For me, there's really no such thing as a typical day. The fishing days, we wake up about 2:00 in the morning, load the boat up with all the ice and all the gear and food and everything for the day. Then we head out. Right now we are fishing about 80 miles out, off the coast. It takes 5-6 hours to get out to the spot. Then we'll lay our lines down. We usually take about 12,000-15,000 hooks with us. It ends up being 5-6 miles of actual baited line and so we put all of that out and wait a few hours. Then we start pulling it back in. It takes maybe 12 hours to retrieve it all. As we are coming back, we're packing the fish on ice, keeping some products alive and sorting through it all. Once that's finished, if everything

"Conservation and regulations are really good things. I think people need to consider that when they think about where their fish is coming from.

Is it possible to eat seafood and do it in a way that helps the ocean?"

goes well – you don't get any hang-ups or sharks don't bite you off or mechanical failures or whatever else happens out there – then you come back in. It takes about 6 hours to get in. Then we unload and sort everything according to species. Every fish has to be weighed and documented. You can do it as a group but each fish has to be in that group. Usually we get in about 3:00 or 4:00 in the morning the next day and the market opens around 5:30 or 6:00. Straight to the market, then finish about noon, rest for a few hours and do it all over again.

Ecologically speaking, when net fishing, you have a lot more byproducts. We can target a certain species based on what it eats, the size of hook we use and the location where we put our lines. If, for some reason, we get hung-up on the bottom or a shark bites the line off and we lose that line, it's not too detrimental. However, if a guy fishing with a net leaves his net, that net is still there and fish can still swim into it. In other words: the net keeps fishing.

The United States is doing a great job of regulating everything, keeping and making sure the stocks are healthy and preventing foreign countries from coming into our waters, depleting our resources. It just really comes down to if people are willing to pay the extra $2 for a wild caught piece of fish and that comes down to the people being educated on what they are eating. That's the only thing that's going to keep us alive, people willing to pay a little extra for a better product. I'm sure it's similar in farming, but with fish you can get the same piece of salmon and if it's wild-caught or farm-raised, you have a 4x price difference. Usually, the consumer is just looking at the price and they don't know why one costs so much more. It really comes down to awareness.

"How can you eat a fish and not know what it looks like?

Try black cod, sable, skate, grenadier, and thorny heads. Ugliest fish in the world, but really amazing."

For fishermen, it's really the best for us to work directly with chefs. When we do, we know that what we just spent hours and a lot of energy working to get will be used. It's not a volume game in fishing anymore, it's about price and quality.

Personally, I have an amazing relationship with the Asian community in my area. They are so passionate about fresh seafood and they buy anything I bring to the dock – that's huge for me because I know I can sell what I have. I know I can sell the guts, the heads, bones, skate, rockfish, whatever, and I know they are willing to pay what that fish is worth. It's an amazing relationship.

A lot of my work is about convincing people to try different things than what they're used to. You know, there are a lot of fish in the ocean that taste similar to cod, but you're probably asking for cod because you know what it is. That's totally understandable. I want people to get away from pieces of swordfish, chunks of tuna, poke, and salmon. I want them to try skate wing, dover sole, sand dow, and all sorts of other fish that have bones and skin and heads on. It's part of the experience.

Buying fish from someone like me means you're getting the freshest fish possible. It's been caught within 24 hours and that's not going to happen unless you come to the docks. Buying wild caught fish means it doesn't have hormones or antibiotics or weird things ground up into fish feed, it's a fish that's been eating what fish should be eating. There's also something important to knowing just how many hands have touched the food you're going to eat. 🌿

"This is the freshest fish possible. It's caught within 24 hours, it's wild cod – no hormones, no antibiotics – who knows what they put in the farm-raised stuff. Here, you know exactly whose hands have touched it throughout the whole process. It's the best natural product you can get."

Paddy Glennon

CLAUSEN OYSTERS;
LOS ANGELES, CALIFORNIA

In a world where chefs create so much of our food culture, Chef Paddy Glennon is an inspiration to many of his peers. Passionate and dedicated to the health and regeneration of our fisheries, Paddy is more than an advocate for change, he's an ally for chefs looking to find integrity in the way they source.

Having committed his life to building a regenerative food system, Chef Paddy is, as he puts it, a champion for the environment, for local fishermen, and for restaurants looking to change.

IN CONVERSATION WITH CHEF PADDY GLENNON

You have to eat the right things. But just because you're eating something that should be the right thing doesn't mean it is. It comes down to sourcing and, honestly, a lot of the time chefs don't really care where it comes from because they need stuff at their back door when they request it.

It's this sort of on-demand attitude that's making it hard to shift the food system we've created. As chefs, we try to inspire our colleagues to work within our food community, to gather what we need to make a meal from within 200 miles of where we live, but a lot of us don't know how to make salt or ferment vinegar. A lot of chefs don't realize what it means to get a fish from an ocean away. It's a lot more than just the carbon footprint, too. It's food safety, human rights, drug trafficking, and so much more.

It's really amazing to see how interconnected everything is when you start to pull back the curtain on our fisheries. A lot of the reason is because we're dealing with open waters and it's hard to keep track of everything that's going on but, for chefs, it's essential that we do. In the United States we have some of the best regulations in the world. Domestically, we have the Magnuson-Stevens Act which protects our oceans, rivers, lakes, and streams from being overfished through regulations set by a scientific quota. We also have between five and seven thousand NOAA on-board advisors making sure that the regulations are enforced and quality control is managed.

> "As a country, we want cheap protein, but cheap protein means it's been fed cheap, hormone, and antibiotic-filled food. That's not good for anyone."

Working in the United States, it's hard because so much of the fish we catch here is immediately exported. In return, we import lower-quality fish because US consumers want cheap, farmed salmon, farmed shrimp, tilapia and swai. They want to walk into a seafood restaurant and order what they're familiar with, not what's in season and that's a huge hurdle for us to get over. For me, working as a fishmonger, it's really difficult to convince a country that imports 92% of its fish to switch to US caught fish. That economic fact makes it hard to convince chefs to put fish their customers might not know on the menu.

You know, when I hear the word "sustainable," I want to puke because it's so overused and abused. The meaning's been lost. We need to champion conscious sourcing that's sustainable, humane, and everything you want it to be from the moment it was caught to the moment it arrives at your back door.

"Education, meals, direct interaction, this is how you do it. If we stay committed, in time, we'll make the change that needs to happen."

It's really hard with fish, more so than just about any other food, because there are a lot of factors not considered. You try to do the right thing and check the rating guides about Red, fish you shouldn't eat; Yellow, fish you can use but it probably has issues with bycatch and feed; and Green, fish that is sustainably caught and you can feel good about everything surrounding it. The problem with this rating system is that there aren't that many Green products.

Another problem with fish, and we've seen this in the industry with other animals, is understanding what to do with the whole animal. Fish doesn't come

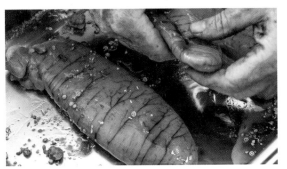

shaped like a rectangle. Rock fish and less familiar species are abundant in our local waters and they can absolutely meet these Green sourcing requirements, we just need chefs and at-home cooks to want them.

I think one of the best parts about working with a local fisherman, if you're a chef in a restaurant, is that of course you get amazing quality, but you also have access. You've got fishermen down on the docks, literally bringing in their catch and texting you with what they've got. You get access to stuff that no one else can get. That's amazing. The problem is that you need to train your customers to want things they might not be familiar with. It comes down to education.

It's hard when you're working in the food industry, especially as the go-between between fishermen and chefs, because the more you learn, the more you start to question what you can eat. Well, what you can eat if you want to eat with any sort of integrity. You have to realize that the expense of flying fish in from Iceland or Indonesia sort of takes away any of its sustainability, especially when you can get fish from your local waters.

I think for the fisheries and the future of seafood, it's going to take chefs like Jason McLeod deciding that they're committed to only sourcing local fish from our local, US-regulated fisheries. Just because chefs might not be familiar with breaking down a whole fish, it doesn't mean they can't learn. Just because their customers always ask for salmon, it doesn't mean they don't want something else. I think that breaking down the barrier between farmer, fisherman, and chef is where the change is going to come. 🌿

"Let the fishermen and the fish dictate the menu."

Jason McLeod

IRONSIDE FISH & OYSTER;
SAN DIEGO, CALIFORNIA

With well over two decades of culinary experience, Chef Jason McLeod knows there's power in volume and purpose in choice.

Believing it's possible for restaurants to source local, sustainable, and conscious seafood, Chef Jason runs a two-Michelin-star restaurant dedicated to supporting our local fisheries. Based in a 1920s era warehouse in San Diego, Ironside runs on oysters and less-than-common fish.

IN CONVERSATION WITH CHEF JASON MCLEOD

When we first opened, Tuna Harbor wasn't open yet, so we called up Paddy and said, "We want to do this right, how do we get the right sourcing dialed in?"

As Paddy says, it's easy to use the word "sustainable" these days, but if you really look around, you're going to see a lot of unsustainable things happening. That's why we try to be as responsible as possible. As a large restaurant group with 13 locations, we do some things that aren't sustainable, but we do everything we can to be responsible.

It actually all started during the build-out of Ironside because I knew I wanted this restaurant to be as good as possible, I wanted to use it as a reason to really learn the seafood industry, top to bottom. Needless to say, that found me on 3:00 a.m. missions up to LA fish markets, making deliveries with Paddy and talking about the real state of the industry. That's when we heard about the possibility of Tuna Harbor, a local dock for fishermen to bring freshly caught fish to, opening in San Diego and I immediately wanted to know how I could support the project. It's fortunate that I have the economic drive of a large, high-volume restaurant, because when we chose to support this project, it gave it viability.

When we first opened Ironside, we thought ordering local fish meant ordering from Mexico, and we thought we were doing the right thing. Then we got educated and we learned how important it is to support US fishermen abiding

"My style is simple, honest, no fuss. I love following chefs from around the world, seeing how passionate, creative, and artistic they are. It's so inspiring, and I spend hours pouring over cookbooks, but I always keep it simple. I like to let the ingredients talk."

by US regulations. They have some serious struggles but they are doing it responsibly and that's something we want to support.

It's not easier to do things how we're doing it. We order a lot of fish, so when you get a whole 250-lb fish in your kitchen, that means your chefs have to know how to break it down and process it. That's a lot of time and a lot of manpower. But, in the end, you're getting a better product, you're supporting people you know, and you're bettering your community. That makes it worth the worry at 1:30 a.m. when you're making orders.

What we've learned is that getting all our fish from the local fishermen is actually a lot easier now. It just took us learning a new method and a new model. Now it's the quickest thing we do. The fishermen text us what they have so we know what's coming in, and that's way better than what we ever had with the big sourcing companies.

> "Local fishing has become the soul of Ironside. We would not be who we are without the fishermen and I think they're doing better because of us, too."

We know the person this fish is coming from, we know how, where, and when it was caught, and we get the whole fish. That means we get to train our chefs how to use it and we have so much more fish to utilize. At first, it was tough, but when we didn't know what to do with something, we called the fishermen and asked them how to use it. I remember calling and saying, "Look, teach me how to cook opah. I want to use it. It has to be a great fish, but I don't know what to do." He broke it down for us and now it's an amazing offering in the restaurant.

> "People think local is expensive for some reason and that's really not true."

For me, the story of local is finding ways to come together. Without that, we're all going to fail. Honestly, buying local is actually easier in the end. You know what you are getting, you have a relationship and that's the biggest part. Without that relationship there's nothing in it. Coming together in conversations is how we do better. Having fishermen ask us what they can do better as fishermen makes our job easier and it goes the other way, too. They call Ironside on Saturday after the market closes and say, "Look, I've got X amount of fish and we need to sell it." And they offer a discount and they know we'll take it all because we can sell it. We don't cherry pick, that's not the game we're in.

"We used to have so many guests that were really upset about salmon not being on the menu. Like, so upset that they left the restaurant. Then people got mad about locally and responsibly caught thresher shark from San Diego. It just took education because we definitely don't get those complaints anymore."

92% of the seafood we consume is imported and less than 1% of that is inspected by anyone. As a country, we export most of our high-omega fish to China and Japan and they, in turn, send us tilapia, swai and farmed salmon – fish deficient in the nutrients we need while being high in what we don't.

MONTH

March

CHEFS

Paddy Glennon, Clausen Oysters & Jason McLeod, Ironside Fish & Oyster

PURVEYOR

Dory Fleet Fish Market

Waking up early to visit the docks, all of the fish for the evening was sourced from the Dory Fleet in Newport Beach, California. Stephanie Mutz dove for uni off the coast of Santa Barbara, and all of the fish offered was pull-line caught, minimizing any risk of bi-catch.

The journey of sustainable seafood is one of the least discussed topics in the slow food movement. Wrought with politics and regulations, it's undeniably a complicated topic, but by committing to local fisheries, it's an easy step forward.

"There's a saying in the sea urchin industry that if you see sharks, you're not working hard enough."

– STEPHANIE MUTZ

TO START

Opah breastplate pastrami

Albacore conserva

Romanesca stuffed pacific squid

Crabby Steve's rock crab
and garden salad

MAINS

Stephanie's sea urchin menudo
with grass fed tripe

Cob roasted black gill cod from
West Caught Fish on South Coast
Farms potatoes and braised greens

CRABBY STEVE'S ROCK CRAB

Serves: 4-6

1   large rock crab, shell removed

1   fennel bulb, with top

2   bunches Bloomsdale spinach, cleaned and washed

5   oranges

¼ cup   olive oil

1   garlic clove

1   shallot

1 tsp   honey

15   basil leaves, roughly torn

3 Tbl   chives, finely chopped

-   salt and pepper

Pick fennel frond from fennel bulb and save for later. Remove core from fennel and discard. Slice fennel thin. Remove peel from 4 oranges and discard. Fillet orange segments from each orange.

DRESSING: Finely dice garlic and shallot. In a bowl, squeeze the juice from the remaining orange. Add garlic and shallots. Whisk in honey and olive oil. Season with salt and pepper and add finely chopped chives.

PREPARE SALAD: In a large bowl add spinach, orange segments, sliced fennel, and torn basil leaves. Drizzle with dressing, mix well, and adjust seasoning. Place crab meat in a bowl, pour a little dressing onto meat, mix, and add a little salt. Place spinach mixture on large platter, top with crab meat, and garnish with fennel fronds.

OPAH BREASTPLATE PASTRAMI

1 opah breastplate trimmed (these average about 3-5 lbs each)

3 qts water

1 cup kosher salt

1½ cups raw organic sugar

1 head garlic cloves, minced

5 bay leaves (we are guilty of planting these everywhere we live in Southern California)

1 Tbl whole coriander seeds (we let our cilantro grow out to seed)

1 Tbl whole mustard seeds (we forage for our wild mustard seeds during our rainy season where we get fields of wild mustard)

½ cup local honey

½ cup ground coriander

4 Tbl medium coarse black pepper, freshly crushed

4 Tbl smoked sweet pepper powder or paprika

5 lbs mixed dry fruit wood and hardwoods (I like a combination of cherry, apple, and oak)

- water to soak the wood chips 2-3 hours ahead of smoking

- wood or charcoal as needed for your personal smoker to smoke the wood chips

KEY TO RECIPE SUCCESS: This takes five days, so prepare in advance. The opah pastrami is best served right out of the smoker but chilled is good too.

BRINE: Once all ingredients are organized, you are ready to make the brine. Fill a medium-size stock pot with the three quarts of water. Add your salt (we make all our own salts from our local ocean blue water, collected 20 miles offshore in open ocean, that we dehydrate down to flavorful local salt), organic raw sugar (can substitute brown sugar), local honey, bay leaves, coriander, mustard seeds, and chopped garlic. Place the stock pot on the stove over high heat to bring the liquid mixture to a boil. Stir occasionally to help dissolve the salt and sugar. Remove the stock pot from the stove and add three quarts of ice to the liquid to cool it. Stir to make sure all ingredients are well mixed to infuse the flavors.

In a container that will hold at least two gallons, place the opah breastplate and pour the cool liquid over the top. Place uncovered in the refrigerator. If the liquid is still warm place the container in the refrigerator until it is cool before adding the opah breastplate.

Allow the opah to brine in the refrigerator for five days. Flip the breastplate daily top to bottom and stir the brine to make sure the flavors are not concentrated on the bottom.

DRY RUB: Mix the coriander, black pepper, and smoked pepper together. Remove the opah breastplate from the brine and lightly rinse it under cold water. Do not rinse for longer than one minute. Pat dry with a clean towel. Evenly coat the breast plate with the dry rub ingredients top, bottom and sides.

SMOKER: Get your smoker started with the method for smoking wood chips needed for your equipment. We use our homemade cob oven with hardwoods we let burn to low ember, before we add our soaked chips.

Place the opah breastplate on your smoker rack and cook slowly, adding wood chips along the process to keep the smoke rolling. Try and keep your smoker below 275°F and cook the opah until you reach an internal temperature of 140°F. At this point, turn off or stop feeding the smoker, which should bring you to the final desired temperature of 145°F.

TO SERVE: Slice the opah breastplate pastrami in ¼-inch slices and lay out the slices on a lovely serving platter. We serve this with pickled vegetables and some homemade mustard. It is awesome in salads or even opah pastrami reubens!

POLE AND LINE ALBACORE CONSERVA

3 lbs   pole and line albacore
        tuna (can be substituted
        with ahi or big eye tuna)

2 cups extra virgin olive oil

2 cups white wine vinegar

    8   cloves of garlic, split
        lengthwise into quarters

    8   bay leaves

1 cup   Italian parsley, chopped

1 tsp   chili flakes

3 tsp   flaked salt (can sub
        with kosher or medium
        course sea salt)

1 tsp   fresh ground pepper

Bring an 8-quart pot of water to a boil. Place 6-pint canning jars along with bands and lids in the boiling water for one minute. Using tongs, transfer the jars, bands, and lids to a kitchen towel on a counter and let air dry.

Clean the albacore of any skin and blood lines, and cut into one inch by one inch cubes, roughly the same size. Place cubed albacore in a stainless steel or glass bowl. Add the salt and toss until mixed evenly. Set aside.

In a small saucepan over medium heat, bring the olive oil, vinegar, garlic cloves, chili flakes, and fresh ground peppercorns to a soft bubble (this is to infuse the flavors). Remove from the heat and add the chopped Italian parsley. Let the liquid cool to room temperature before adding to albacore. Mix softly until the fish is evenly coated.

Pack the albacore in the jars leaving about 1-inch room at the top of each jar. Try to make sure each jar has at least one clove of garlic. Distribute excess liquid evenly in each jar. If the liquid does not cover the albacore in the jars, top with additional olive oil so the albacore is just covered by a bit of oil at the top. Gently tap the sides of the jars to make sure the liquid settles evenly between the albacore chunks. Wipe clean the rims of the jars with a warm, wet towel. Seal the tops with the lids and screw on the cap bands.

I use this method when I am serving the jars right away at our farm dinners or if we will be eating the Albacore Conserva in the next few days. Try to always serve them close to room temperature. Either serve them from cooking, or if you cook the jars a few days ahead, pull from the from cooler a few hours prior to serving so the flavors are not reduced by the cold.

Place a pastry glazing rack or canning rack on the bottom of a large stock pan large enough to place all jars flat on the bottom. Add enough water to cover the height of the jars by 3-5 inches. Bring the water to a boil. Using rubber lipped canning tongs, lower the jars one by one onto the rack. The water should easily cover the tops of the jars. Bring the water back to a boil and cook covered for 30 minutes. Remove the jars from the water and place on a counter with a towel underneath. The tops will most likely "pop" in the centers as they start to cool.

Serve with the top off with a spoon and some crusty bread!

SEA URCHIN MENUDO
with grass-fed tripe

Serves 8

8 live, California sea urchins

2 lbs grass-fed beef tripe

2 lemons, juiced

1 smoked pork hock, quartered

2 fresh bay leaves or 1 dry

½ chili pequin pepper, crushed

3 Tbl chili powder

1 small white onion, chopped fine

1 Tbl fresh garlic, chopped fine

½ tsp ground cumin

30 oz organic white hominy

½ tsp fresh oregano

2 lbs frilly seaweed (or use rock salt to hold the uni steady)

MENUDO: Cut tripe into bite-size pieces, place in large bowl, add lemon juice and toss to coat evenly. Chill for one hour to tenderize. Drain and rinse, and place in a large 6-8 quart cooking pot or slow cooker. Add smoked pork hock, bay leaf, chili pequin, and enough water to cover the tripe. Bring the liquid to a boil, and cover with a lid. Reduce heat to medium-low and cook menudo, covered, for four hours.

When tripe is tender, add chili powder, onion, garlic, cumin, hominy, and enough water to replace any liquid that has evaporated. Simmer menudo for 30 minutes and season with salt and black pepper.

PREPARING URCHINS: Using clean garden gloves or kitchen towel, hold the urchin with the beak/mouth outward. Using a serrated knife, place the blade on the upper side just behind where the shape of the shell (beak side) goes from flatter to curved. Saw through the sea urchin until the top comes off and discard.

Using a small spoon, gently remove the orange/yellow urchin tongues from inside the shell and place them in a bowl. Remove all the blackish connective tissue and discard (this goop is great in your garden). Clean the inside of the shell with a soft sponge and running cold water.

Place a bit of seaweed in the bottom of individual soup bowls, just enough to keep the shells from tipping over. Gently pull off any connective blackish tissue from the urchin tongues and place 3 tongues in each urchin shell. These are now ready for the menudo service.

TO SERVE: Bring the menudo up to a nice simmer. Blend the remaining urchin tongues with ½ cup of cold water to a puree. Add the urchin puree to the menudo and stir. Ladle the menudo into the serving bowls in front of your guests and have them sprinkle a little fresh chopped oregano on top. Enjoy.

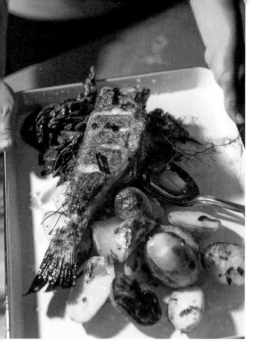

ROASTED BLACK GILL COD

with fennel and potatoes

2	whole local rock cod, head and inners removed
1	fennel bulb, roughly chopped but even
15	sprigs thyme
3	bay leaves, torn
1 lb	tiny potatoes, cut in half
4	garlic cloves, sliced
6	shallots, rough chopped
1	lemon, sliced
1	whole lemon
-	sea salt
10	basil leaves, torn
1 cup	extra virgin olive oil

Season the fish generously with salt inside and out and rub with a little olive oil. In a bowl, add fennel, potatoes, thyme, bay leaves, garlic, shallots, lemon slices, ½ cup olive oil, and a good pinch or two of salt. Toss mixture well.

On a baking sheet covered with foil, evenly spread fennel and potato mixture. Place fish on top of vegetable mixture.

Place in 350°F preheated oven (or a cob oven if you have one) and cook for 20-25 minutes. Remove from oven and place fish on a platter. Remove vegetables from baking sheet and place on a serving tray, sprinkle with beautiful sea salt, olive oil, and a generous squeeze of lemon juice and top with torn basil leaves.

TIP: Don't be afraid to use your favorite herbs or vegetables that you grow in your own garden.

ROMANESCA STUFFED PACIFIC SQUID

Serves 8

48-64 whole US squid, fresh

2 cups romanesco broccoli or broccoli cooked "al dente" in boiling salted water

2 cups fine bread crumbs

1 sweet onion, diced fine

1 Tbl garlic, chopped fine

½ cup white wine

1 cup fresh basil, chopped fine

1 cup fresh Italian parsley, chopped fine

1 cup extra virgin olive oil

3 large eggs, beaten

½ tsp salt

½ tsp black peppercorns, freshly ground

- toothpicks as needed to pin each squid

2 pints fresh tomatoes, pureed with skins and seeds removed

1 pint roasted peppers, pureed with skins and seeds removed

½ cup onion, finely chopped

1 tsp garlic, finely chopped

½ cup extra virgin olive oil, divided into two ½ cups

STUFFING THE SQUID: Remove the tentacles from the body. In the center of the star of their legs is the beak of the squid. Pop this out and discard. Chop the tentacles finely and set aside from bodies. The easiest way to clean the body cavity is to press between your fingers from the tip of the squid in the direction of the mouth of the cavity. You can also lay them flat on a cutting board and roll them out with a rolling pin. What you will get out is the ink sacks (they may break open and that is OK, no harm here!), the entrails, and some jelly-like substance which can all be discarded or composted.

Add ½ cup olive oil to a large sauté pan over medium-high heat. When hot, add chopped tentacles, salt and pepper. Sauté for two minutes on high, stirring gently. Transfer the cooked tentacles to a mixing bowl.

In the same sauté pan over medium heat, add the rest of the olive oil and sauté onions until translucent. Add garlic and sauté an additional two minutes. Deglaze the pan with the white wine, gently stirring to release the natural caramels formed from cooking. Add this mixture to the tentacles and let cool.

Add remaining ingredients and adjust seasoning to taste. Using a toothpick, stab a small pin hole in the tip of each squid to let air escape when stuffing. Fill each squid body ¾ full using a pastry bag. Close each squid with a toothpick.

COOKING THE SQUID: In a medium saucepan over medium heat, sauté onions in ½ cup olive oil until translucent. Add garlic and sauté another two minutes. Add pureed tomatoes and pepper puree, bring to a boil and reduce to a simmer.

In a separate large pan over medium-high heat, add the remaining olive oil and gently sauté stuffed squid in batches for another two minutes on each side. The squid will shrink slightly and some stuffing may be pushed out. Add the sautéed squid to the tomato/roasted pepper liquid. (If the squid release a lot of liquid, discard this liquid from each batch, wipe pan clean and start the sauté process again for the next batch.) Simmer the squid in the sauce on low heat for 20 minutes.

Remove the squid from the pan. When they are cool enough to handle, remove the toothpicks from each squid. Strain the liquid from the cooking pan through a medium strainer. Reduce the liquid by about ⅓ to coat the serving plate with.

Serve the stuffed squid on serving platters. Sprinkle a little extra virgin olive oil over the top and garnish with sprigs of fresh Italian parsley leaves or fresh basil.

REMOVE CONTAMINANTS AND
TOXINS FROM OUR FOOD SUPPLY

Choose
Organic

Organic is about using a more biological approach to how we grow our food. How can we be more in alignment with the natural way of things? It starts by removing toxins from every part of our food system.

Choose Organic

THE ESSENCE OF FARMING
HAS ALWAYS BEEN ORGANIC

It all starts with healthy soil and healthy soil demands non-toxic methods. Meaning: the synthetic fertilizers, pesticides, and fossil-fueled herbicides developed post WWII for conventional farming are actually contaminating, not sustaining, our food system.

> "Organic is about a belief in a
> biological approach to how we
> grow food."

Understanding that nature is not a factory, and that conventional farming is the result of a societal preoccupation with both efficiency and the novelty of technology, is key to this principle. Understanding that farming is *meant* to be organic, it's designed to be non-toxic, and it is possible to grow food at scale, in a natural way. We've grown food for thousands of years without toxins, we don't need them now.

When we "Choose Organic," ultimately, we support farmers with not only integrity but a common belief in the harmony of nature. We see a connection between our healthy body and a healthy planet – if we do not ingest fertilizers and pesticides, why should we spray them?

If the essence of farming is about soil, healthy food is about healthy soil. Conventional farming sacrifices the beneficial biology native to our soil in service of the bottom line and a higher yield. Every single time we spray the land, we're killing the organisms that are essential to its health. While farming organically does not necessarily build healthy soil, it is certainly the first step.

The word "organic" only had to start being used a few years ago. Prior to that, everything was holistic, it was always in alignment with nature. Historically, our farming methods used animals to manage the soil without the use of pesticides or other man-made interference.

"Choose Organic" is absolutely not a deep dive into sustainable agriculture. We purposefully put it near the beginning because understanding what organic is and isn't is really an integral starting point. So what is organic? Organic does not include a Genetically Modified Organism at any point in the process; it does not use synthetic fertilizers, pesticides, chemical additives, or non-organic herbicides; and it does not use sewage sludge. So if that is organic, that means its counterpoint, "conventional agriculture," does include genetically modified organisms, fertilizers, and sewage sludge as part of its process.

> "*Conventional* is one of the
> greatest marketing schemes
> we've ever seen."

Our regenerative food future starts with a foundation of organic practices, one where we don't have to choose between conventional and organic; from a place where organic is the standard and small-scale farmers have the opportunity for economic viability, resulting in multiple small farms in a community.

Ideally, this future separates the purchase of produce and commodities. In other words, supermarkets sell organic food and farms will sell produce. The acts of gathering and consumption will shift toward something more special, sacred, specific, and purposeful. Ideally, this shift to a foundation of organic and separated points of purchase will happen not only on a retail level, but with restaurants and hotels as well. Restaurants, chefs, and the commercial industry as a whole have higher purchasing power than individuals, meaning their sourcing choices potentially create greater economic viability for the farmer.

The draw of a more organic, old-world approach, celebrating craft and art, has been growing since the 1970s. Seeing the rise in vibrancy and accessibility of farmers markets, of consumer interest in sourcing and production, and the commitment of chefs to sourcing transparency, all points to organic becoming a mainstream expectation.

> "You shouldn't buy your dry goods, produce, and toilet paper in the same space."

The belief that our food can, and should, be grown at any time of the year, anywhere in the world, and shipped

wherever we want it, has led to our current state of disconnection. The next step, once organic is the new standard for production, is to shift the equations we use to think about food. Meaning: tomatoes do not have to be part of every salad, bananas and pineapples do not need to be purchased in December, and we do not have to have a fear of variety in our diets. Just because it's edible doesn't mean that's how nature intended it.

When considering ecological agriculture, organic means that we're working toxin-free. It does not mean

we're actually farming in a holistic, ecological manner. Again, it just means we're toxin-free. But that's the first step to a healthy food system. We have to get the toxins out of our food and our soil before we can really start regenerating our planet. Once the toxins are out, we can start to integrate deeper and more meaningful practices.

UC Santa Cruz is the heart and center of the sustainable agriculture movement on the West Coast, and Allan Chadwick, an early organic gardener from England, brought a host of really important ideas and garden techniques to Santa Cruz in the mid 1960s. Starting an organic garden on a south-facing slope full of poison oak and brambles, he transformed it into one of the most important organic gardens in America. It became the classroom for thousands of the leading organic farmers in the world, and it still sits as a four-acre model for how to grow food with integrity, moving far beyond just non-toxic production.

Gardens like that are what inspired The Ecology Center to be a point of conversation in Southern California. We believe offering tactile visuals for the community to interact with is key in the shift toward organic as our primary practice of agriculture.

"How you share your message is just as important as your message."

Unfortunately, Orange County doesn't have many examples of great organic agriculture in our backyard. However, The Ecology Center is located on one of the only certified organic farms in Orange County and George Kibby, our neighbor, has been farming 26 acres in San Juan Capistrano with his wife, Rebecca, for the past 20 years. They've built a community around organic food – from a thriving farm stand to a beautiful CSA program full of delicious seasonal produce grown on site. George's commitment to organics is unwavering because he, like us, knows it is the absolute building block of healthy agriculture.

Simply distilled: to grow healthy food, we have to have healthy soil and healthy soil is not full of toxins. ✿

Choose organic, buy local and demand products with a story of integrity.

HOME

Know the Dirty Dozen (conventional foods with the most pesticides): strawberries, apples, nectarines, spinach, cucumbers, cherries, bell peppers, peaches, celery, grapes, tomatoes, and cherry tomatoes.

Remove all GMO products from your pantry

Use organic soil when potting plants and growing vegetables

RESTAURANT

Remove GMOs from the kitchen (including canola and soy)

Commit to purchasing as many organic products (both produce and dry goods) as possible

Build relationships and source from farmers who practice organic growing methods

George Kibby

SOUTH COAST FARMS,
SAN JUAN CAPISTRANO

Farmed by George and Rebecca Kibby, South Coast Farms is a 26-acre farm nestled in San Juan Capistrano, near a train station, the historic district, and less than two miles from the beach. As one of the only certified organic farms in Orange County, Farmer George has been stewarding his land organically for over 20 years as an urban, not rural, farm in Southern California.

The land of South Coast Farms has been farmed for 140 years, seeing a neighborhood build up around it. As a small-scale local farm, South Coast Farms is an ideal model for a transitional solution to the future of farming.

Growing both commercially and direct to consumer, South Coast Farms has a thriving farm stand and a robust CSA program. Their direct to consumer model gets the best local, seasonal, organic produce into the hands of local residents while giving the farmer a down payment in advance for his harvest. Investing in the local economy like this makes small-scale organic farming a viable option for farmers because they now have the capital to invest on seed, labor, and future growth.

As the only working certified organic farm in Orange County, California, farmer George of South Coast Farms had a challenge, not only as an urban farm, but as a farmer in general. Turned on to farming in high school by a family friend, he studied, read up, and worked at a dairy before quitting school to buy a small plot of land and grow some strawberries. Thirty-five years later, he has a thriving organic farm in the heart of Southern California.

IN CONVERSATION WITH GEORGE KIBBY

A lot of people worked very hard, for a lot of years, to have the word "organic" represent value in the marketplace. If you follow those guidelines, you deserve to reap any rewards from the use of the word organic.

"Buying direct from the farmer minimizes packaging, branding, and overhead. The cost is lower and the benefit is higher."

Legally, it takes three years to become a certified organic farm; practically, it's a lifelong process trying to understand the biology, chemistry, and physics of the soil, water, amendments, and seed genetics you're working with. To be honest, I don't really know that much about non-organic farming, but I can say none of my workers are exposed to dangerous chemicals and the food we grow can be eaten straight from the fields, at any time of day. I don't really think too many non-organic farms can do that.

Organic farming is hard because we're facing a lot of challenges that don't just exist in the field. Most of the battles we're fighting aren't about whether or not people want organic food, they're about compliance with the Food Safety Modernization Act, known as FSMA, that's coming down the road. It's with Good Agricultural Practices third-party certification and, honestly, it's with the extreme influx of cheap Mexican organic produce coming across the border.

For me, the hardest challenge is cheap organic produce from Mexico, because they are able to pay their laborers $10 per day, without any added social cash cost. In California, we not only have to pay a fair wage, but we have added costs like workman's compensation insurance, state and federal taxes, unemployment insurance, and more. That adds up to around $20 per hour, per worker. That's a far cry from $10 per day. So if they can meet requirements for USDA NOP Organic, of course their organic produce will be exceptionally cheaper than California-grown organic.

There's also just environmental conditions you have to deal with, too. To cope with the drought in California, we water less, choose planting dates differently,

"There are real challenges and practicalities to organic farming. It isn't just one thing over another. There's a business to it and there's also water, hard work, and if anyone actually wants your tomatoes or not."

and hope we get some rain in the winter. In reality, though, Southern California is always in a drought so it is not really the drought that's an issue, it's the cost of water that's really the challenge.

In 2005, the city of San Juan Capistrano departed from the usual business model where water districts purchase their water from upstream providers. Instead, they decided to build a water treatment plant, using their own groundwater to supply a new reverse osmosis plant. This resulted in the loss of the water well the farm had always used and we got put on municipal water. Making a long story short, agricultural water has a lower rate than municipal water. So when we got put on municipal water, we began paying a far higher rate for our water. It's a challenge, but we do our best to try and find some sort of solution. 🌱

"Water is always a challenge. In San Juan Capistrano, it's a huge hurdle and there doesn't really seem to be a solution."

Flemming Hansen & Mette Helbæk

STEDSANS IN THE WOODS; HYLTEBRUK, SWEDEN

Chefs Mette and Flemming create beautiful food that's clean, simple, and shared lovingly. Their style is as much Californian as it is Danish, always starting with the ingredient and building from there.

As the only international chefs at Community Table, Mette and Flemming are an inspiration for the interconnection of local zones across the world. Before they closed their restaurant, Stedsans Østegro, in Copenhagen to move their family to a homestead in the forests of Sweden, eventually opening another food experience, the duo had one of the most enviable kitchens in Denmark. At only 600 square meters, Stedsans was a rooftop farm in the middle of the city, just past a fitness shop and up a set of fire stairs, designed for 25 guests at a time. Almost impractically, the greenhouse had two gas burners, two chefs, and offered two seatings of 25 a night.

Serving family-style food, Flemming and Mette source nearly all their ingredients locally, focusing on quality and seasonality. Interested in the botany of food and its medicinal purposes, Mette grows many of the ingredients for their restaurant and, as Flemming says, though he may not be a trained chef, it's easy to make good ingredients taste beautiful.

Chefs like Mette and Flemming with their commitment to clean, simple, organic food are an example for the future. As chefs everywhere begin to transition kitchens from conventional operations to a more local approach, we need models for how to do it.

IN CONVERSATION WITH METTE HELBÆK

For us, Stedsans is about a sense of place, not just geographically, but a sense of place in time, the land, and each other. I grew up in a home where every meal was home-cooked, we never had takeout and those tastes became the

"What tastes better is better, always. The food that comes from a farmer who builds back his topsoil tastes better than one who does not. There's more care and better energy put into it."

foundation for me as a chef. I still remember that those meals were about making us feel good, nourished, and happy. That's what we try to do every time we feed someone. We want you to feel cared for, because that's what the act of sharing food is about.

Flemming and I met in 2002 when he had just started his first restaurant and I was studying at university, but I had been bitten by the food bug a long time ago and I could never stop thinking about it. I've always worked with it in lots of different ways, from styling to food writing, cookbooks, being a restaurant critic, to selling local-only organic produce. Eventually, we started Stedsans on a rooftop in 2013.

It really is all about the ingredient. That always comes first, whether we're cooking at the restaurant or having lunch at home. I think it's easy to get inspiration from Mother Nature because, if you go with the seasons, the ingredients all have a different story when they come to your table from the fields. They speak to you in ways that tell you a story about how they want to be used.

I remember at Flemming's first restaurant, he got most of his vegetables from local farmers, specifically this one farmer named Søren Wiuff. Søren has since become very famous in Denmark, but he used to come late at night with bags of vegetables and herbs straight from the farm and they made us want to cook, right there, in the middle of the night. We wanted to turn on the burners, pull out the bowls, and begin to cook.

> "With a few changes, it is possible to meet produce demands with sustainable choices. We have to demand it and we have to keep talking about it."

TIPS FROM METTE HELBÆK

Daily Inspiration
Denmark has such clear seasons that it's easy to be inspired by the nature around me and its changing seasons. For quick inspiration, I love Instagram and Pinterest, seeing what other people are doing and how they're showing it.

Kitchen Essentials
Every kitchen should have a spoon for tasting and stirring, a sharp knife, a big pot and a chopping board. That's really all you need but a pair of scissors for clipping herbs is quite nice, as well.

Get Outside
I never feel better than when I cook outside. When we were traveling through California, our best meals were enjoyed around an open fire, surrounded by a forest of big redwood trees.

It's really amazing to me how little you have to do if you have good ingredients. Showing off how amazing Mother Nature is, is pretty easy, but it's also easy to forget how extraordinary the world is when you shop at ordinary supermarkets.

I think it's essential to approach food with the understanding that we are all one, and we should act accordingly about that. If people could just realize that what you do today impacts you tomorrow, we could change the world really fast.

Of course, at the restaurant, our relationship with farmers means everything to us, but it should for people at home, too. Growing food, or even just sourcing locally, it helps tie you into the different stages of a plant's life, the different seasons of the year, and the real work that goes into growing one piece of food.

Any serious chef has to care about sustainability because it's how we make the ingredients better. If chefs just decide to commit to only sourcing organic and local ingredients, whenever possible, it's possible. The challenge comes in making that choice a continuous priority.

The future is about sharing. Whether it's ideas, sourcing, photos, inspiration, seeds, whatever – the world needs us to share. Growing up cooking, it became the most important skill I ever learned, and I am so grateful to share it with my children. I want them to know how to take care of their health, how to make people happy and satisfied, and how to break free of the industry around food. It's empowering.

"We always try to give back more than we take."

January

Flemming Hansen & Mette Helbæk, Stedsans in the Woods

South Coast Farms

Clean and simple food, shared lovingly.

Chefs Mette and Flemming brought the heart of their rooftop greenhouse-to-table restaurant in Copenhagen, Denmark, to California, with family-style plates, beautiful local ingredients, and first of the season strawberries.

Quietly powerful, without compromise of quality or community, Stedsans is 600 square meters, with two chefs, two burners, and two seatings of 25 a night.

"We've seen that the people who come to eat clean food and sustainable food are really good people.

If we have very, very good ingredients, then it's simple to cook. I'm not a trained chef, but I know how to make good ingredients taste good. That's pretty easy."

– FLEMMING HANSEN

FIRST

Strawberry and goat cheese salad with balsamico

Raw veggies with smoked sour cream and homemade crackers

Roasted cauliflower, browned butter, almonds, apricots, arugula, and parsley

MAINS

"Krebinetter" Danish pork patties with carrots, onion, and cabbage

Grilled romaine with blue cheese, walnuts, and grilled citrus

LAST

Lemon mousse with cream, chocolate, and navel oranges

STRAWBERRY & GOAT CHEESE SALAD

with balsamico

Serves 4-6

1 cup balsamic vinegar

2 Tbl honey

1 lb large strawberries, stemmed and quartered lengthwise

½ lbs chèvre style goat cheese, crumbled

- black pepper, freshly ground

¼ bunch of fresh cilantro, rinsed and stems removed

In a medium pan, heat balsamic vinegar and honey on medium-low. Allow to thicken until mixture resembles syrup, about 15-20 minutes. Set aside.

Place the strawberries on a tray. Add freshly ground black pepper to taste. Drizzle strawberries with the balsamic reduction, crumble goat cheese over strawberries, and garnish with cilantro.

GRILLED CAULIFLOWER

with brown butter and apricots

Serves 4-6

1 lb	organic butter
1	Meyer lemon, halved
2	medium heads of cauliflower
10-12	dried apricots, diced
2 cups	arugula
¼ cup	salted almonds, crushed
-	sea salt
-	black pepper, freshly ground

1 lb	almonds
2 tsp	sea salt
-	a few drops of water

Heat a medium pot on medium, add butter and allow to brown until golden and nutty in flavor, about 15-20 minutes. While butter is browning, heat a medium pan on high. Place lemon flesh side down and dry panfry until lemons are aromatic and dark brown. Once butter is brown, squeeze in lemon. Set aside.

Heat a grill on high. While grill is heating, remove excess leaves from cauliflower heads. Grill whole, until al dente, about 10 minutes. Remove from grill and cut into quarters. Add sea salt and freshly ground black pepper to taste.

Stagger cauliflower on a medium serving platter, and generously drizzle brown butter over the cauliflower. Sprinkle arugula in the empty spaces of the platter, then top with apricots and almonds. Add sea salt and freshly ground black pepper to taste and serve.

SALTED ALMONDS TO ACCOMPANY: Preheat oven to 300°F. Mix together almonds, salt, and water and place on a medium baking tray. Bake in the oven for 15-20 minutes, until the almonds are completely dry. Serve alongside Grilled Cauliflower with brown butter and apricots.

GRILLED ROMAINE AND ORANGES

with walnuts and blue cheese

Serves 4-6

1 large head of romaine lettuce, quartered into wedges

2 oranges, halved

2 Tbl olive oil

- sea salt

- black pepper, freshly ground

½ cup toasted walnuts, crushed

3 oz wedge of Pt. Reyes Blue Cheese (or similar), crumbled

Heat grill on high. Once hot, place romaine on grill, and cook until each side is slightly charred with visible grill marks, about 3-5 minutes. Set aside.

While romaine is grilling, place orange wedges face side down on a small pan set on medium-high. Cook until orange is aromatic and flesh is dark brown, about 3-5 minutes. Set aside.

On a large family platter, place the grilled romaine, drizzle with olive oil, and squeeze one half of the grilled orange over the top of each wedge. Add sea salt and freshly ground black pepper to taste. Sprinkle with walnuts and crumbled blue cheese. Serve with remaining orange halves.

HERBAL TEA

from the garden

Serves 4

We used:

2 bunches fennel tops

2 orange slices

5 sprigs of sage

3 sprigs of mint

32 oz hot water

We recommend mixing and matching whatever herbs are in your garden or available at your local farmer's market, and steeping them in hot water, about 10 minutes.

SEED CRACKERS WITH SMOKED SOUR CREAM
and raw seasonal vegetables

Serves 4-6

¾ cup flax seeds
¾ cup chia seeds
1 tsp dried fennel seed
2 tsp sea salt
1½ cups water

16 oz full fat organic sour cream
½ lb apple wood chips

6 medium radishes,
cut lengthwise

6 medium turnips,
cut lengthwise

½ small head of red cabbage,
cut into large bâtonnets

10 snap peas

- nasturtium for garnish

SEED CRACKERS: Eight hours (or more) before serving, mix together chia seeds, fennel, and salt. In a non-reactive bowl, soak seeds in water until water is consumed and the seeds are soft to the touch and gelatinous. Spread a thin layer of the mixture on a parchment-lined full baking sheet, and bake for 1-1½ hours at 400°F. Crackers should be firm and crispy. Set aside.

SMOKED SOUR CREAM: Soak wood chips in water for 2 hours before use. Heat grill on high. While grill is heating, poke 10-20 small, pin size holes in a medium tin foil tray, and place chips in tray. Once grill is hot, cover the wood chips with another tin foil tray. Once chips are aromatic, remove from heat, pour sour cream in a small heat-safe bowl, and place with the chips. Cover well and allow to sit for about 20 minutes. Sour cream should taste smokey.

TO SERVE: Arrange vegetables on a small plate. Sprinkle with crumbled chia seed crackers and serve with a dollop of smoked sour cream. Garnish with nasturtium flowers.

"KREBINETTER" WITH STEAMED VEGGIES

(Danish breaded pork patties)

Serves 4-6

2 lbs	organic ground pork with 22-25% fat (ask your local butcher)
1 cup	buckwheat
-	sea salt
-	black pepper, freshly ground
1 cup	ghee (or butter)
4	medium white onions, skin removed
8-12	medium carrots, tops removed
1	small oxheart cabbage, quartered
1 lb	butter, cubed

Preheat oven to 400°F. Form ground pork into softball-size patties, add sea salt and freshly ground pepper to taste. Coat each side of the patties with buckwheat. Heat a large pan on high. Once hot, reduce heat to medium-high, and add in half of the ghee. Working in batches, place patties in pan and panfry until each side is brown and buckwheat is golden, about 5-7 minutes. Finish in the oven, about 5-8 minutes. Once done, meat should reach a temperature of 145°F and hold for four minutes. Cover and set aside.

Place whole onions on a medium baking sheet, and cook in oven for about 20-30 minutes until fork tender. Skin should be brown. While onions are cooking, in a medium pot, add cubes of butter between layers of carrots, and steam until al dente, about 5-7 minutes. Do the same with the cabbage. Add sea salt and freshly ground black pepper to taste.

Place the vegetables on plates, top with krebinetter and drizzle with pan drippings. Serve.

LEMON MOUSSE & CITRUS COMPOTE

with shaved chocolate

Serves 6-8

4 cups	heavy whipping cream
4 cups	Greek yogurt, drained
2 Tbl	pectin
2 Tbl	boiling water
1	lemon, juiced and zested
1 cup	organic cane sugar
2	medium cara cara oranges, segmented
2	medium blood oranges, segmented
2	medium navel oranges, segmented
½ cup	shaved chocolate or cacao nibs

In a large bowl, beat heavy whipping cream until it has medium-soft peaks, about 4-6 minutes. Set aside in a cool place.

In a separate, non-reactive bowl, mix together pectin and hot water. Once incorporated, add in lemon juice, zest, and sugar until smooth, and stir in drained Greek yogurt. Gently fold in whipped cream. Do not over mix. Mixture should be light and fluffy. Pour mixture into 6-8 glass canning jars and allow to chill in the refrigerator for at least four hours.

Top with raw segmented oranges and shaved chocolate, and serve.

ONLY EAT ANIMALS RAISED
WITH INTENTION AND RESPECT

Respect Animals

Animals are the key piece to regenerative agriculture. If you can't find animals raised with integrity, choose to opt out.

If we should raise animals is not the question, it's *how*. After all, we are responsible for their well-being, from birth to death and on the plate.

Respect Animals

ANIMALS ARE A KEY PIECE TO REGENERATIVE AGRICULTURE.

Design your flock off nature. Use the whole animal. Practice holistic management and positive animal husbandry. When considering the holistic management and positive husbandry of animals, the most responsible thing we can do is truly commit to not only using the whole animal but to only purchasing meat that's in season, local, and has been raised with integrity.

Animals are a natural part of the fertility cycle. They create manure which fertilizes the soil, providing nutrients for vegetables and other plants. When they're pastured, they not only offer management of the vegetation, but they offer a delicate destruction of the landscape. When managed properly, hoofed animals can be used to churn the soil, create beds for seeds, and pollinate the land. We can and should put animals to their best use as stewards of the farm and our food system.

"In a society that eats meat, we need people willing to raise meat in a beneficial — not depleting — way."

In Southern California, the more common approach to husbandry is difficult because of a lack of precipitation, but — as always — one should design one's flock off nature. Considering the natural patterns of animals, we can watch the buffalo stampede in close quarters from prairie to prairie. They do not stay in a paddock until it is destroyed, they delicately destroy the landscape and then move on so it can regenerate. When we raise our animals, we should do the same.

Celebrating use of the whole animal, especially in culinary, is essential. We must recognize because of the hard work it takes to raise animals well, we need to patron restaurants with chefs who work creatively to use the whole animal, and we should, at home, do our part to support our local economy. Why? With a local

economy that produces local food, we are able to repopulate our food system. This results in a vibrant, realistic culture. Just like we cannot only have our favorite season (we have to have four), we cannot only have our favorite (or most familiar) cuts of meat. Sometimes we have to get creative, we have to make concessions, and we have to realize every piece is part of the whole.

Animals are integral to a healthy farm ecosystem; they always have been and they always will be. As stewards of our landscape, animals provide the incredible function of fertility and land management. Moreover, they offer important economic and culinary products. From eggs to meat and cheese, animals are essential.

This is not a conversation about whether we should or should not raise animals, it's a conversation about

how we raise them. Animals provide us with so many amazing things, the least we can do is care for them with love and respect.

> "We have to love our
> goats, sheep, chickens, and
> pigs as much as we love our
> dogs and cats."

Currently, the way we bring animals to our plate is cruel, industrial, and inhumane. If we raise animals healthfully, they make our land healthier which, in turn, makes our food and planet healthier. Animals were not designed to eat corn, hormones, grain, and seed. They are meant to eat seasonally, and primarily herbaceous material. Since that's the case, how can we expect them to taste delicious if the very food we're giving them is inedible?

We have to ask the cost at which we've designed our conventional system of animal husbandry. Yes, it's convenient and efficient for the mass production of meat, but is it possible to design a system that's instead celebratory of a healthy community and healthy ecosystem? If we did, we would see dynamic grazing patterns that model wild animals.

"Eat smaller portions, less frequently. Animals and their meat should be celebrated and respected."

Practically speaking, raising animals with respect means we have to redesign not only our farms but our relationship to animals as a whole. How can we treat them well, providing the right size pastures at the proper rate of rotation? Interestingly, if we give animals the right and diverse types of food, paired with a

culture of care that honors humane and organic practices, we can raise less animals with the same yield. We care for our animals from birth to death and respect them accordingly on the plate. We believe we need to not only minimize our production of animals, but our consumption as well. The goal is to raise our animals locally, with ranchers we know, who have integrity and share the principled commitments we believe in. Ideally, we buy directly from these farmers at markets, through cooperatives and local butchers.

Respecting animals is a commitment, because if we cannot find sources of meat that share our values, we have to opt out. That might mean seeking a full-time vegetarian diet, it might mean going vegetarian once a week. Either way, both are incredibly beneficial, regenerative, and kind to the environment. 🌿

Buy off-cuts. Make stock. Use things you've never heard of. Enjoy exploring. Talk to your butcher.

HOME

Consider meat as a side, not a main

Support your local butcher and experiment with different cuts than you're used to

Choose meat that is hormone-free, antibiotic-free, and pasture-raised sources for meat, dairy, and eggs

RESTAURANT

Remove meat from your menu at least once a week

Support producers who can give you the quantity you need but that also have the best practices

Challenge yourself and team to use all parts of the animal, like making your own stocks from bone, etc

Includes not just conventional animals, consider fish, game, and the like

Krystina Cook

COOK PIGS RANCH,
JULIAN, CALIFORNIA

Cook Pigs is a family operation, raising heritage pigs on pasture, surrounded by live oaks and the rolling hills of inland San Diego County. Feeding the pigs a vegetarian diet of local, seasonal foods, Cook Pigs harvests wheat grass from their neighbor, seasonal avocados, fallen macadamia nuts, Julian Mash apples, and additional seasonal vegetables grown on the farm and nearby.

Selling only whole pigs, their commitment to using the whole animal underscores their belief that farmers should be leading chefs.

IN CONVERSATION WITH KRYSTINA COOK

We started raising pigs about eight or nine years ago when I realized I had some food allergies and needed to look at my diet. That, eventually, led to looking at our larger food system as a whole.

Back then, we began with about four pigs, all Yorkshire-Duroc crosses but we were, and still are, a working farm so we don't just have pigs. We usually have at least one or two of all the typical farm animals because things tend to work a lot better together. It's funny, but it really makes it easier.

For us, when we're raising our pigs, we truly want to take care of them. Right now, one of our sows is farrowing – which means having babies – and her litter is about five days old. We try to take care of her just as much as all the others. They all need good food and something to play with and that's really part of the craft it takes to raise good pigs. It's an art, it's not just raising pigs.

When we started, we looked at our location first. Asking, *How can we raise pigs well in Fallbrook?* We realized we had a lot of things happening in our favor but also a few limitations, ultimately, that led us to exploring a macrobiotic diet for them. Depending on your location, what you raise your pigs on and how you do it will – and should – be different. The principles, though, should always be

"We've always been focused on quality and now it's more about craft."

around good food and a stimulating environment. For us, that meant feeding our pigs food from the area, things like avocados and grains and fatty nuts.

As with anything, the more you do it, the more you start to develop preferences. For us, we were raising our pigs and, though we'd started with Yorkshire-Duroc crosses, we eventually created our own heritage breed after four generations. They're known as Cook's Breed and are a cross between Yorkshire-Duroc (Hampshires) and Red Waddle (Andrus Breed). We then bred those with a Glaushire Old Spot, which we then bred with a Hampshire, resulting in Cook's Breed.

Of course you want a big pig, but we aren't looking to raise fat pigs. We're ideally looking for no more than three inches of fat because we want more protein, not fat. This means that when we're looking at our pigs, we want to see lines, we want to see fat and heartiness, but we also want to see tone.

Because we let our pigs roam, we sort of think of them like kids: we raise them up to a certain weight and then let them fend for themselves. They all have individual personalities, particular likes and dislikes, but in general they can all be happy if they're given some play and good food.

"It's funny, people think pigs are pigs, but they really have sensitive bellies. We shifted our pigs to a soy free and almost corn free diet pretty quickly."

It's really important for us to share our practices with people because that's the only way that what we're doing will become the norm. We want people to know that our method is economically viable and worth their time. We want to them to understand that things like having a relaxed and happy pig is important because then they're not releasing hormones that spoil the meat, so you're actually able to sell it at a higher price.

At the end of the day, though, it's always about relationships – and not just with our pigs. It's about the restaurants and the consumer. They're the ones who make what we do possible and we want them to know why our pigs are better for the environment, better for them and better for their customer. It's all a cycle.

It's funny because the way we do things at Cook Pigs is at once looking back and forward at the same time. We originally picked Julian, California, because its climate is so close to Spain and Portugal, where Jamón Ibérico and black pigs are produced. But we're also so far ahead of where our food system is. We're constantly gathering information about better ways for us to farm, for chefs to use our pigs, and we're always going out of our way to refine our craft. We want to be in dialogue with people because that's what's going to help us change people's mind about how they spend their dollars.

I cannot really consider myself a rancher. I raise a gorgeous craft product that's different than anything else. I've put in a lot of time and a lot of hours to be the only one doing things the way I do in Southern California. I raise forested pigs under old growth oaks, finished on nuts, fed a seasonal diet – no one is doing that. But I want them to. 🌱

"Our pigs aren't for everyone. We aren't trying to hit the lowest common denominator. These pigs aren't for the supermarket because we don't believe in that model."

Michael Puglisi

ELECTRIC CITY BUTCHER;
SANTA ANA, CALIFORNIA

As a butcher from New York, Michael Puglisi has worked in Boston, Miami, and Los Angeles, cooking and butchering in restaurants, to learn about their local food systems.

Through it all, he has become obsessed with sourcing transparency and direct access to excellent produce. As the founder of Electric City Butcher in Santa Ana, California, Michael has a heart for excellent meats that have been bred, raised, and processed with the greatest care and quality.

IN CONVERSATION WITH MICHAEL PUGLISI

I went to northeastern Sicily with my wife to visit a cousin who runs the only butcher shop for his small village. It's so interesting because he is totally supported by the people of his community, and that support allows him to be particularly familiar with the meats he sells. He's able to process the meats – hide, tripe, tongue, liver, every single bit – exactly to how he wants to. When people come into his shop, they don't ask for something; they tell him how many people are coming to dinner; he comes back with a hunk of meat or a chicken and that's what they're eating tonight. They're having what the butcher says is the best part, and the whole community is working to eat the whole animal together, not just the parts they favor. This transparency doesn't happen in the States. It's getting there with fruit and vegetables right now, but not with meat.

I've always been a butcher at heart – I love charcuterie, the application and transformation of an animal is something I'm fascinated with – so encouraging a barrier between the rancher and the consumer, it doesn't make sense to me. They work too hard raising this meat for us to cut and wrap and put it in a box. There's no reason our entire meat system has to be like that.

"That's what I wanted to do with my shop. I wanted to bring back these traditional food systems. You see that happening everywhere with food, but not with the butcher shop."

At Electric City, we aren't organic, we're just responsible. We consider everything: the feed, carbon footprint, handling, health of the animal, breed, age, where it comes from, the farm – all of it – so we can truly feel we have found the most responsible source.

It's interesting because our farmers do not participate in the organic certification process. They are natural, sustainable, hormone-free, antibiotic-free, and are good, clean, healthy animals raised in pasture. You don't have to pay for a certification to tell us what the right choice is. Again, it's about transparency.

Thinking about meat in terms of seasons is really interesting, and you mostly see it in pork and beef. During the winter months, beef is more marbled because the grass is much more abundant and they're eating more of it. Same thing with the pigs – in the summer, you see them a bit leaner because they don't like to eat in the heat, and they forage less. You also see a little fluctuation with the density of the meat, it's a little bit looser. So, when we open animals up in July, we'll notice they may be thin on fat, yet the meat eats the exact same way as pork or beef in the winter because of the flavors. The textures change slightly, but not much, when they're living in the right environment. This is what happens when animals eat what and when they're supposed to eat, not when they're artificially bulked up on supplements.

I think one of the greatest testaments we have to the quality is the lack of fluctuation in flavor from our farmers. They might have a little difference in color, density, or marbling, but it always eats the same. That's consistent quality.

Replicating our model of cut-to-order, extremely high-quality whole animal butchery isn't easy. But the guests to our shop live close by and they want to see us succeed. They want that relationship, they want to build trust with their

"That's what we need most: clean, healthy animals that are thriving in their environment because then they can get what they need nutritionally, and we don't have to add chemicals and steroids to their diet. It's simple. Or at least it should be."

butcher. They want their meat ground right in front of them and, since we don't have anything to hide, that's how we do it. You can see straight into our walk-in from across the street, and that level of transparency is time consuming, but it's worth it!

Educating people on supporting whole animal usage – which doesn't mean you have to eat every ear and snout, it means you don't just order the rib-eye of a cow because there are a lot of other cuts – that's what we have to do. We need to make sure that someone knows how to correctly cook the piece of meat they just bought; sometimes we need to encourage them to try something new. I can teach someone how to cook duck just by talking to them, and then they come back saying they need more duck. It's phenomenal.

There are more and more local butcher shops opening around the country, but it's important not to lose your way or compromise integrity. We struggle with that a lot, and I ask myself every day, "How do we make cut-to-order butchery more accessible?" Something I'm most proud of is that we're a whole animal butcher shop, and we take our trash out every day with one hand. We literally do not let anything go to waste because we have the talents to take care of the animal, to preserve it, process it in the right way. I feel that we're mandated to care for that animal that died for our use. And it's a very humbling thing to truly use the entire creature to its full potential, respectfully.

Our meat is special. The way it's raised, the way we handle it, the way it's enjoyed by our guests at the dinner table. That's what this is all about for me. The relationship to our food and how it makes us feel. ❧

"It's true what they say – you are what you eat. So if the pigs are eating acorns and fallen peaches, you taste that, you really do... Whatever's on the ranch, that's what the pigs should eat. It's not as romantic as the pigs only eating acorns for three months in the fall, but the natural way of things just works better."

Ryan Adams

370 COMMON;
LAGUNA BEACH, CALIFORNIA

Known for his creativity in the kitchen and dedication to unexpected pairings, Chef Ryan Adams loves to experiment with ingredients, creatively learning how to waste less.

This usually means giving a second life to things that are often scrapped, trying out new techniques, and generally discovering "waste" is not often waste. The result is intimately interwoven flavors and textures, deeply thought-out menus, and very little excess.

IN CONVERSATION WITH CHEF RYAN ADAMS

I grew up in a family that cooked a lot. I watched my grandmother a fair amount and she was an excellent cook. Watching her really showed me this old-school style of preparation and cooking. That's what I want to be. I want to use every-thing, utilizing all the parts – even the inedible ones – so that nothing makes its way to the trash. The way I look at it, if there's something that goes in the trash, I'm making a mistake.

It's funny to think about now, but when I was a kid, my punishments were always something around cooking, or tending to the garden, picking lemons, something like that. Let's just say, I had to make a lot of bread dough and pick a lot of beans. Since I was a picky eater, too, my grandma and mom eventually just told me I could start cooking for myself if I didn't like what they were making, so I did.

It's interesting to watch people, because a lot of folk talk about doing certain things, but when it comes down to actually buying a product or doing some-thing, they don't. They aren't out there walking the walk, they're just talking the talk. That's something that gets me riled up because I want to make sure I'm really doing the things I say are important. It's a point of pride for me to source locally and to use as much of a product as I can.

"For me, nothing gets tossed. I can compost and use scraps. There just shouldn't be waste."

One of my favorite things to emphasize with the younger chefs I work with is how to utilize everything. It comes down to learning what a quality product is and how to consistently deliver that.

I love working with farmers and ranchers like Cook Pigs because they do things in ways that have been used for hundreds of years. They aren't doing anything new, they're just modifying the details to fit their region and specific needs. And that's amazing. When you can use methods that have been perfected over decades, chances are, you're going to do it really right. You can taste that.

So when you're raising animals, this sort of care is essential. When you subject any animal to stress, they are going to release the hormone cortisol and cortisol makes meat taste terrible. It also makes the animal gain weight and fat in the wrong places. That's why when you look at conventional pork, you can see how much fat is on that meat and it's not a beautiful, marbled sort of fat, either. It's just fat. If you compare that to someone like Cook Pigs, you can literally see the difference in the meat. Their pigs are more meat than fat, but they've been raised on such a delicious diet that the meat itself is rich and full of flavor. They raise these pigs at a 5,000-foot elevation and feed them local apples, nuts, avocados, and they're happy. These happy pigs deserve to have every single part of them used and, selfishly, as a chef you want to make the most of what you have.

"You have to make the time to do things the right way. You're probably going to have to give up doing something else, but make the time. Figure it out."

It's interesting because using the whole animal really asks you to be more creative and more keen with your techniques. It's easy to make the "good" cuts taste delicious, but it often takes a little more care to use the less sought-after parts of an animal. Like, it's not as easy as just throwing salt on and grilling it, you know you can't put certain cuts over direct heat, you need to think about muscular fat, and you have to be aware of what some things are going to do. You have to just treat it a little different and, to be honest, that's a lot of the fun.

When I source, I look for what's in season and what I can try to use every part of. I really like to think about things as interwoven and unexpected. For my dinner, I was so excited to get this principle, this season, and this purveyor. Fall and winter are my two favorite times of year to cook because you have to stretch. Your ingredients aren't as abundant as summer and you have to be okay with switching things around and changing things out.

Something I'm really proud of is that we did a Tahitian squash where we roasted it and really worked to pull the sweetness out. We couldn't find butternut squash, so we had to pivot, and I really like making calls like that. I like finding flavors that push against one another – like dandelion against squash or chicarron against vinaigrette. It's so fun to make them tie together, pulling certain elements from one into the other. Like, think about using the braising liquid from the meat so you can emulsify your vinaigrette. That's so much fun. Honestly, though, it really comes down to taking the time to think it through. That's all it is. ✿

"Some cuts are tougher than what people are used to, like the shoulder and the butt because well-raised animals are building muscle because they're moving around. It's a simple trade-off for flavor, though. Whatever you have to give up in tenderness, you make up for in flavor."

MONTH

November

CHEF

Ryan Adams, 370 Common

PURVEYORS

Cook Pigs Ranch & Electric City Butcher

Drawing on the essence of pine, the rich fats of seasonal nuts, ripe avocado, and late-season apple, Chef Ryan Adams cooked over an open fire, burning wood from Cook Pigs, tying everything together with a little smoke.

Embodying a sense of time and place, this meal feels like fall.

"Ingredients can have many lives and this is part of cooking the natural way. The heart of seasonality is to not waste; it's to find uses for everything. One thing bleeds into the next, blurring hard lines so everything becomes a progression, offering the opportunity to not only think creatively but intelligently about how to use our resources."

– RYAN ADAMS

FIRST

Wood roasted Tahitian squash salad, apple pork vinaigrette, blue cheese, and candied walnuts on dandelion greens

Pine-cured Cook Pigs terrine with mustard seed, persimmon, water-cress, and bread

Cider-braised pork belly with wheat-grass, Meyer lemon, and carrot

Mushroom-stuffed pork loin with parsnip, potato, escarole, and persimmon

LAST

Pear galette with lemon verbena, crème fraiche, honey, and squash seeds

MUSHROOM-STUFFED PORK LOIN
with roasted parsnips & fingerling potatoes

8 oz	maitake mushrooms, chopped
1	garlic clove, finely chopped
1 Tbl	fresh parsley
1 Tbl	fresh thyme
1 Tbl	shallot, sliced
1	pork tenderloin
2 Tbl	olive oil
-	kosher salt and black pepper

2 lbs	fingerling potatoes, washed
6	parsnips, peeled and cut into ½-inch pieces
2	heads escarole, washed, trimmed, and quartered
1 tsp	garlic, chopped
1 tsp	kosher salt
½ tsp	black pepper, ground
¼ cup	olive oil
4	sprigs of thyme

PORK LOIN: Sauté the mushrooms over medium heat with the olive oil, ½ tsp of kosher salt, ¼ tsp pepper, sliced shallot, and garlic. Cook until soft. Remove from the heat and stir in the thyme and parsley. Let cool.

Cut the pork across (not all the way through) lengthwise so you can open it like a book. Pound the meat with a mallet until it's about ½ inch thick. Cover the pork with the mushroom mixture and starting with a long side, roll up the tenderloin and secure with toothpicks. Rub the outside of the pork with salt and pepper. Bake in the oven at 385°F for 25-30 minutes or just until pork reaches 160°F. Remove from pan and let rest 10 minutes before slicing.

ROASTED PARSNIPS AND POTATOES: Combine all the ingredients except the escarole and toss. Place onto a sheet pan and roast at 400°F for 30 minutes, stirring every 10 minutes. After 30 minutes, stir in the escarole and roast for another 10 minutes. Remove when complete. Serve sliced pork loin on top of vegetables in a platter, family style.

PINE-SCENTED PORK TERRINE

with pickled mustard seeds on toast

1 cup	onion, finely chopped
2 Tbl	unsalted butter
2	garlic cloves, finely chopped
1 Tbl	fresh thyme, chopped
1 Tbl	kosher salt
-	spruce tips, dried
1 tsp	black pepper
¼ tsp	ground allspice
¼ tsp	nutmeg, freshly grated
1	bay leaf
½ cup	heavy cream
2	large eggs
3 Tbl	whiskey
½ lb	chicken livers, trimmed
1½ lb	ground fatty pork shoulder or half lean pork and half fresh pork fatback (without rind)

1 cup	yellow mustard seeds
1 cup	plain rice wine vinegar
¾ cup	distilled water
½ cup	mirin
½ cup	sugar
1 Tbl	kosher salt

PINE-SCENTED PORK TERRINE: Cook onion in butter in a sauté pan, covered, over medium-low heat, stirring frequently until soft, about 10 minutes. Add garlic and thyme and cook for one more minute.

Transfer to a large bowl set in a bowl of ice to cool. Meanwhile grind spruce tip, salt, peppercorns, allspice, nutmeg, and bay leaf in a spice grinder until finely ground. Add to onion mixture and whisk in cream, eggs, and whiskey until well combined. Next pulse chicken livers in a food processor until finely chopped, then add to onion mixture along with ground pork and mix together well with your hands. Line bottom and long sides of terrine mold with plastic wrap. Fill terrine evenly with ground-meat mixture, tapping terrine on counter to compact it (it will mound slightly above edge). Cover top of terrine with excess plastic wrap and chill at least overnight to marinate.

Preheat the oven 325°F low fan. Cover terrine tightly with a double layer of foil. Bake terrine in a water bath until thermometer inserted diagonally through foil at least 2 inches into center of terrine registers 155-160°F, 1¾-2 hours. When complete, remove foil and let terrine stand 30 minutes. Next place the terrine in the mold on a sheet pan, place another same-size terrine mold or a piece of wood or heavy cardboard cut to fit inside mold and wrapped in foil. Put 2-3 (1-pound) cans on terrine or on wood or cardboard to weight cooked terrine. Chill terrine in the refrigerator with weights until completely cold, at least 24 hours.

PICKLED MUSTARD SEEDS: Combine all ingredients together in a small saucepan and bring to a gentle simmer over low heat. Cook until the seeds are tender, about one hour. If too much liquid evaporates, add just enough water to cover the seeds. Cool and store in refrigerator for up to one month.

TO SERVE: Slice terrine and place slices on toast. Top with pickled mustard seeds.

THYME ROASTED TAHITIAN SQUASH

1	Tahitian squash, peeled, seeded, and cut into 4-inch pieces
¼ cup	olive oil
1 Tbl	kosher salt
¼ tsp	black pepper, ground
3	sprigs of thyme

Preheat the oven to 375°F. In a large bowl, toss the squash with the olive oil and thyme and season with salt and pepper. Spread the squash on a baking sheet in a single layer and cover with foil, then roast in the oven for about 40 minutes until tender and lightly browned. Serve warm.

APPLE CIDER PORK VINAIGRETTE

½ cup	extra virgin olive oil
¼ cup	warm pork fat
¼ cup	raw apple cider vinegar
2 Tbl	maple syrup
2 Tbl	Dijon mustard
¼ tsp	black pepper, freshly ground
-	pinch salt

Whisk together the olive oil and vinegar. Add the remaining ingredients and whisk (or shake in an airtight container) vigorously until well combined. Hold in a warm water bath until service.

CANDIED WALNUTS

⅓ cup	maple syrup
1½ cups	raw walnut halves
⅛ tsp	coarse salt

Preheat oven to 350°F. Lay walnuts out on a baking sheet in a single layer. Bake for 5 min. Test for doneness. Be careful not to burn. Remove from oven and let cool in pan on a rack.

Preheat a dry skillet over a medium-high heat. Add walnuts, maple syrup, and salt. Cook, stirring frequently, until syrup is caramelized and nuts are toasted, about 3 min. Spread the walnuts on a baking sheet, lined either with a non-stick mat or parchment paper. Use two forks to separate the walnuts from each other, working very quickly. Sprinkle the nuts with salt. Let cool completely.

CIDER-BRAISED PORK BELLY

with apple glaze & homemade sea salt

4 lbs	pork belly, cut into 8-oz pieces
3 cups	apple cider
2 cups	chicken stock
1	stick cinnamon
12	whole allspice berries
4	whole cloves
2	carrots, peeled and cut into 1-inch pieces
2	stalks celery, cut into 1-inch pieces
1	medium onion, peeled and cut into eighths
	2 cloves garlic, peeled and halved lengthwise
4	fresh bay leaves
1 Tbl	sea salt
-	black pepper

1 gallon	unfiltered organic apple juice
2	fresh bay leaves
¼ tsp	cracked black pepper
1 Tbl	lemon juice

1 gallon	super clean sea water (check local beach quality reports or get a fisherman to get it from open waters)

PORK BELLY: Score the fat side of the pork belly ¼-inch deep in a crosshatch pattern and season liberally with salt and pepper on both sides. Place pork belly in a medium pan, fat side down. Place the pan over medium heat and cook until golden brown, about 10-12 min. Turn and sear for an additional 8-10 min.

Preheat convection oven to 300°F. Bring the cider and the chicken stock to boil in a Dutch oven over medium heat. Once boiled, remove from the heat and add the cinnamon, allspice, cloves, carrots, celery, onion, and garlic. Stir to combine and add the pork belly, fat side up. The liquid level should be just below the top of the pork belly. If not, remove some stock. Cover and bake for 3½ hours. After 3½ hours, uncover and continue cooking for 30 minutes more.

Remove the pork belly from the oven, discard the aromatics and save the braising liquid (chill and freeze for another use). Heat the apple glaze (recipe below) over medium heat and add the pork belly, two pieces at a time, turning with tongs to coat thoroughly with the glaze, season with sea salt and serve.

APPLE GLAZE: Combine all ingredients except the lemon juice together in a small saucepan and bring to a gentle simmer over low heat. Cook until large bubbles begin to form, then remove from heat. Add the lemon juice and stir. Cool to room temperature and hold until needed. Store in the refrigerator for up to one week. Bring to room temperature before using.

SEA SALT: Strain seawater through a coffee filter into a large stock pot. Bring the water to a boil then let cool. Next pour the water into a large rimmed pan and place into a super low temperature oven to start the drying process. Salt will start to form on the edges first. Turn the oven off when this happens and let the pan cool in the oven. If you have a gas oven, just leave the pan inside. The pilot light will provide enough heat to finish it. Be sure to move the salt with a fork until done to the desired texture. Remove from the oven when cool, wrap the pan with cheesecloth and place in a sun soaked window to finish the drying process.

To serve, plate with apple glaze smeared beneath and on top of pork belly, then sprinkle with sea salt.

PEAR GALETTE
with crème fraiche & candied squash seeds

1¼ cups	AP flour
2 Tbl	sugar
¼ tsp	baking powder
¼ tsp	salt
⅛ tsp	baking soda
5 Tbl	butter, cut into ½-inch cubes and frozen
¼ cup	cultured buttermilk, plus 2 Tbl more

1	large egg white
3 Tbl	confectioners sugar
2 tsp	melted butter
3	firm, ripe pears, such as anjou or bartlett, cored and sliced ¼-inch thick
2 Tbl	fresh lemon juice
1½ tsp	grated lemon zest
¼ cup	granulated sugar
¼ tsp	cinnamon
2 tsp	butter, cut into small bits

2 Tbl	maple syrup
2 Tbl	packed brown sugar
¼ tsp	allspice
¼ tsp	salt
1 cup	shelled pumpkin seeds

2 cups	heavy cream
3 Tbl	buttermilk

PASTRY: Pulse flour, sugar, baking powder, salt, and baking soda in a food processor for 30 seconds to combine. Add butter. Pulse until butter pieces are the size of peas. Add buttermilk and pulse until dough just comes together. Form dough into a disk, dusting lightly with flour. Cover in plastic wrap and refrigerate minimum one hour.

FILLING: Whisk egg white and sugar in a bowl until frothy, then drizzle in the melted butter. Set aside. In another bowl, combine the pears, lemon zest, and lemon juice and toss together.

Lightly dust a sheet of parchment paper with flour. Place pastry dough on top and lightly dust with flour. Top with another sheet of parchment and roll out dough into a circle about 12 inches in diameter. Peel off top layer of parchment. Invert dough onto a baking sheet lined with third sheet of parchment. Trim around edges of dough. Spread egg white mix over dough, leaving a 1-inch border. Pile pear slices in the center over egg whites. Sprinkle with sugar and cinnamon. Evenly scatter bits of butter over top of filling. Fold edges of dough over pears, crimping dough to enclose ends of pears. Bake at 400°F for 20-25 minutes or until pears are tender and crust is golden brown.

CANDIED SQUASH SEEDS: Preheat oven to 350°F. In a small saucepan, combine all of the ingredients except the pumpkin seeds. Heat over medium, stirring constantly until brown sugar is melted and mixture is frothy. Then add pumpkin seeds and stir until coated. Once complete, spread pumpkin seeds on greased sheet pan and bake for 10 minutes, stirring every couple of minutes. Remove from oven and cool completely. When seeds are still warm stir them to break up clumps.

CRÈME FRAICHE: Add the heavy cream and buttermilk to a mason jar, screw the lid on tightly and shake. Remove the lid, cover the top with cheesecloth and set out at room temp 70-75°F for 24 hours. Once complete, remove the cheesecloth, screw the lid back on and place in the refrigerator for 24 hours before use.

Serve galette sliced and topped with candied squash seeds and crème fraiche.

PARTICIPATE IN THE ACT
OF GROWING FOOD

Grow
Your Own

Growing your own food is not only
delicious, it's empowering. Today, it's
a revolutionary act, but what if our
communities were to become food
forests instead of sidewalks with
lawns? Let's grow vibrant landscapes
full of food and a connection to nature.

Grow Your Own

FOOD DOESN'T COME FROM THE SUPERMARKET,
IT'S GROWN, AND IT CAN BE GROWN ANYWHERE.
WE SHOULD PRACTICE THAT.

Growing a healthy food community is possible, no matter where you live. Every community can turn their backyard into bounty, their sidewalks into herb gardens, and their lawns into food forests. We believe the experience of food is meant to be shared and that coming together around a table full of things freshly harvested and simply prepared is healthy. Moreover, it sets the scene for thinking creatively about solutions while inviting people into a positive loop of giving and receiving.

Growing food does not have to be hard and deconstructing that idea is our first step. We think it starts with what "landscaping" is – why don't we grow food instead of lawns? Why don't we share our extra harvest with our neighbors? If you don't have access to good ingredients, can you begin by growing? By having a garden in your backyard, or even just an herb garden, you're able to remove the middle man by providing yourself with direct access to good food. This is the starting point for a vibrant food community. We all have to begin somewhere and since we can all grow food, that should be where.

I started to realize the garden was something special when I began gardening with my mom as a kid. It took until college to start growing food but, once I did, everything changed. Somehow the act of growing something essential to our human experience made me

feel like I had the capabilities and potential of the entire world at my hands. The possibility was infinite: I could grow anything and that knowledge changed my life.

I dove in. I went head first, straight to the deep end, transforming my backyard into a thriving garden. Ultimately, gardens became the platform through which I'd meet like-minded people, enamored with food and growing it. In college, we had a backyard farm, we worked on farms, and we turned our lives, into a culture of gardening. I think tasting and touching it made all the difference. I mean, walking down the street to pick strawberries, driving up the coast to pick tomatoes, it leaves an impact.

> "Let the food speak for itself. Use great ingredients and don't mess with them too much."
>
> – GREG DANIELS

For me, spending the rest of my life with food and growing it was going to be the core of who I was and what I did. I know that some people see gardening as a reach, but it's fundamentally harmful to spend too much time in industrialized society and urban environments without some sort of true, honest connection with nature. Fortunately, the easiest way is through gardening.

Gardening is not just a joy, it's also edible food and the best-case scenario: you put in work and you get something you need out of it. Plus, it's incredibly easy because you can truly garden anywhere. Additionally, it's accessible because you do not need a lot of money to do it. In fact, if you live in a food desert, growing your own food can actually be a huge benefit.

> "Gardening is beautiful and enjoyable. It's also super functional and very practical."

It's important to remember that growing a garden doesn't have to be intimidating. You don't have to go all out with the perfect backyard garden or not do it at all. It really is as simple as starting small and building

a connection to nature and food. That's it. It can be an herb garden and that's amazing. Maybe you eventually add in a little veggie box of lettuces. One day, a lemon tree might find its way into the mix and, maybe, on the far end, you eventually have a full homestead. Really, anything from a couple herbs to absolutely everything is possible and perfect.

Start somewhere, start small, and start simple. The process doesn't have to be an overnight thing. One of the best parts about garden culture and growing your own food is that, yes it's delicious, but it also comes with an amazing community. Gardeners and growers want to share their passion and they want to connect. That's just as much part of the harvest as whatever veggies you're pulling out of the ground.

For us, at The Ecology Center, we're transforming lawn culture into a rich, vibrant garden culture. We think lawns work much better as food forests mainly because we can be more connected as communities.

It's that simple. The more connected we are with nature and each other, the better we are for it. So when we start to pull up our lawns and get our hands in the soil, we experience an amazing reconnection.

One day, our communities will be entirely transformed into holistic ecosystems but it starts with deciding that we don't want to pull into our garages and close off our doors, having the gardener come to mow the lawn.

We have to start asking ourselves what kind of community we want to live in and just because we can't see what we want now, doesn't mean it can't happen. We want to see big, beautiful, established trees lining our streets because we think a key indicator for a healthy community is shade. Having shade and having pride in our landscapes makes us want to spend time outside, connecting with nature.

Ideally, most gardens should have a section dedicated to the kitchen. Hopefully, there are a few fruit trees in there, too. Eventually, we want our local cities to see value and health in their communities having gardens over lawns.

"The goal is to connect with nature and to connect with your food and that can happen a lot of different ways."

Gardening is not a privileged benefit. It's one of the biggest weapons we have as citizens because we have the power to grow our food, liberating us from the control of big business.

It's important to remember that gardening and creating ecosystems starts with education. ❧

Start small, keep it simple.

HOME

Get yourself and your
kids in the garden – build
veggie boxes or find a
local community garden
where you can rent a plot

Commit to seasonal and
organic growing practices,
harvesting and eating the
food you grow

Extend the harvest
through food preservation
techniques; canning,
pickling, drying

RESTAURANT

Grow your own culinary
herbs, at least. Hire
young local farmers
to maintain your
restaurant garden

Feature the vegetables
and produce you grow
on your menu, make it
a talking point

Encourage staff to attend
gardening workshops or
to visit the farmers you
source from

Evan Marks

MARKS HOMESTEAD;
OCEANSIDE, CALIFORNIA

As founder and director of The Ecology Center, Evan Marks constantly uses his background in permaculture and agroecology. Having worked extensively in California and Hawaii, and internationally in Costa Rica, Peru, Mexico, Ghana, and Nigeria, Evan believes people have the ability to directly impact the environment through individual change.

Stewarding a small homestead in Oceanside, California, with his wife Kristin, a textile designer specializing in natural dyes, and their son Ocean, Evan is passionate about the idea of food forests in his own backyard.

IN CONVERSATION WITH EVAN MARKS

Our house is a sacred space and while we sleep there, almost all of our activities are outside and that's because we have beautiful shade. We've consciously designed shade and outdoor living spaces so that over the last year, we've transformed our lot from just lawn to a vibrant ecosystem. All rain that comes onto the property ends up in catchment tanks which then overflow into rain gardens and those rain gardens are the core irrigation system for the native habitat garden in the front of the house.

Around our house, we designed it so that there are trees, all edibles, throughout the property – about 25 fruit trees – and they grow what we like to eat. So we grow certain foods and there is fruit we can harvest every single month of the year: citrus, avocado, bananas, figs, peaches, plums, you name it, it's all there. And we grow a lot of our vegetables. The thing with growing food at your house is about relative location. It's about growing food as close as you can to your kitchen because you're going to eat every day, three times a day. You have to connect things together.

One of the simplest implementations of permaculture in the household landscape is to imagine that wherever your kitchen is, your herb garden is as close

"We have to see things as interconnected, we have to think about solutions, we need to make the changes now. It's possible. Abundance is possible, but it starts with choice."

as you can possibly imagine. So that might be as far as your garden capabilities go but at least you're growing herbs. Your next step is that you're going to have a lemon tree because you can harvest lemons every single day of the year when you have a thriving tree and that goes into your salad preparation, vinegar, and garnish. Then you have vegetables – the vegetables that you harvest all the time, like your greens, are going to be one layer further, then it goes out and you have your produce that you harvest less often. Seasonally, this rotates. Further away from the kitchen is where you'll have things like your compost, which is in connection to your potting bins, which is in connection to a shed which is in connection to a chicken coop.

At our home, we're oriented to the south. South is where the sun is, so you want to make sure your food production is happening in orientation to the south. As a result, you line up your vegetable production and your fruit tree production so that it gets maximum sun exposure. The shade of trees in the summertime will shade your house and when they're dormant in the winter, without leaves, it leaves space for the warm sun to heat your house. Using deciduous trees like this is intelligent patterning of the landscape and you can also use evergreen trees, like citrus. For things like citrus, you want to put them to the north side of the house because they need enough sunlight to grow but they can also block the cold winter winds, keeping your house extra insulated.

The basic eco-kit that we talk about from an infrastructure perspective is about starting small with a raised veggie box. If you can't have a raised box, try a container garden on your patio, followed by a worm bin. Worms are an integral part of the nutrient cycle and compost production of your garden. After that, you want to create a space where you can eat outside and another where you can pot seedlings. Next, maybe you add in chickens. With plants, start with herbs and then veggies, add in fruits and natives after that. The following step would be to include rain barrels. It really is a puzzle when you start getting into the logistics of it all, but it's fun to figure out how everything can work together.

At The Ecology Center, our mission is to model creative solutions for thriving on planet earth – to be part of the solution – and while that sentiment is woven into everything we do, it really takes shape in our Grow Your Own! initiative. We know our future can be abundant, but it starts with teaching our community not just that it's possible to, but *how* to live in alignment with nature. To do that, we have to offer the chance for people to evolve the fundamental framework through which they consider the world. That is the easiest way to make sure our future generations see us as part of (not apart from) nature. ❧

"Food is the one central thing about human experience that can open up both our senses and our conscience to our place in the world."

– ALICE WATERS

"You see the world differently when you start to get your hands dirty."

Megan Penn

ORANGE HOME GROWN;
ORANGE, CALIFORNIA

Backyard farmers are absolutely going to change the world. Whether it's realizing you can grow all the herbs you need, or that you can actually make a profit from the extra zucchini you grew this season, backyard farming has the potential to truly put the power of food back into the hands of the people.

For individuals like Megan Penn, growing food and starting a farmers market came down to will, community, access, and the desire for an empowered experience.

IN CONVERSATION WITH MEGAN PENN

In college at Cal Poly San Luis Obispo, I started raising backyard chickens because I loved the idea of having access to fresh eggs and, at one point, our little house off of Higuera had upwards of ten chickens in the backyard.

After college, I moved back to Orange and reconnected with old friends who were also living in the area and we started meeting around kitchen tables, trying to figure out the logistics of starting a farmers market in our community. This eventually led to the formation of our non-profit, Orange Home Grown. It took two years, but we finally hosted our first official farmers market on May 7, 2011, on the grounds of Chapman University's Villa Park Orchards Packing-house. We have been growing the reach of our grassroots organization ever since through the support of our city, local organizations, and local businesses.

Running a community-driven farmers market takes a lot of people-power. We rely on the kindness of volunteers to support the weekly programs and activities that the farmers market offers every Saturday. The Orange Home Grown board has been the driving force behind the growth and development of the organization. In 2014, we decided that we wanted to provide more locally grown food opportunities to our community in addition to the weekly farmers market. At the same time, I made the decision to leave my professional planning and architecture career so I could step off the board and into the role of the Execu-

"I've always had an interest in gardening. My grandfather had a victory garden with chickens and ducks, so my mom grew up with that. I think because of that exposure, she made a point to always have something growing when we were kids."

"I think the reason I was able to get a farmers market going in Orange was because I had access to amazing volunteers and the kind of people who wanted to help make it happen."

tive Director here at Homegrown. That was a big move and we hired a market manager, plus an assistant market manager, to help us expand the offerings of our market. Knowing that we work hard to create programs and opportunities for people to have a healthy life, both physically and mentally, is something that's so rewarding for me.

From the farmers market came the idea of starting a seed lending library. We paired up with the Orange Public Library Foundation and repurposed an old card catalog, filling it with donated seeds. Once we had the seeds, we needed a place to provide hands-on learning. We paired up with Chapman University once again and started the first education farm in the City of Orange.

"I said to myself, What would really make me happy is if I could do this full-time because this is what fills my soul. This is what makes me tick. Seeing all the positivity it brings is worth all the work. This is what I want to be doing all the time."

I think that if you're just getting started growing food, it's a good idea to begin with a small space and to not be afraid. Try something and, if it doesn't work, there will always be another growing season. After all, vegetables aren't permanent and you can try again.

It's funny, but I think people appreciate things differently now. There is something very interesting about going back to your roots and getting your hands dirty, of trying to do some of the things our ancestors did for generations, like save seeds. These skills aren't brain surgery, we just have to want to know how to do them. It's always easier to go grab seeds at the store or to pick up produce on the way home, but at some point you have to decide that knowing these things and living this way are important parts of the life you want to live.

The Orange Home Grown Education Farm is a 7,000 square-foot, single-family residential lot that's about 120 ft deep and about 60 ft wide. The property

is owned by Chapman University in Old Towne Orange, California. The farm is surrounded by houses and across the street there's a five-story parking structure – it isn't exactly what you'd picture when you're thinking about a farm. Through the support of volunteer power and local business donations, the farm took shape and has grown into a space where neighbors come to volunteer every Friday. We offer monthly garden workshops, community open house days, private farm classes and events, and pop-up pay-what-you-can farm stands.

One of the ways we provide education on the farm is by having people work together on projects as a community. When volunteers show up on Friday mornings, we have a list of things we need to work on and we invite them to help us get it done. A lot of what we do is really fun, like planting and harvesting; shoveling manure and moving compost piles can be more strenuous, but there is always work to be done on the farm.

For me, I love growing food and raising chickens and I want my children to understand how important it is to know where our food comes from. I want them to take care of our earth. I'm also grateful to my mother and grandfather for playing such a role in my life and I hope I can do the same for my daughters.

One of my favorite things is growing food out front, it's like a beacon. People always stop by wanting to know what's growing and it's a wonderful conversation starter, especially when we grew a giant pumpkin. It took over almost our entire front yard and everyone wanted to ask us questions. That's what it's about. It's not about quantity, it's about community. 🌱

"It's not about the money; we're never going to make a lot of money. It's about getting food on people's tables and delivering produce three blocks down the way so people can eat it and become aware of where it comes from."

Greg Daniels

HAVEN GASTROPUB;
ORANGE, CALIFORNIA

Growing up with a love for the restaurant industry, Chef Greg Daniels spent a lot of his childhood at the spots his mom worked for 27 years, taking home suckers and desserts from the chefs after her shift. He always felt at home there, like there was a rag-tag sense of family to the whole thing and, for him, that's how food has felt ever since.

Everyone has to eat so why can't the way we go about it be positive and nourishing? Starting at 15 at the local KFC, Chef Greg Daniels came out of his shell, learning to interact with customers, getting teased by the cooks, and finding the like-minded people he didn't know he was looking for.

IN CONVERSATION WITH CHEF GREG DANIELS

I started out as a bartender and did that for about 12 years, eventually going to culinary school during the back third of it. I think I went to culinary school because there was a ceiling to my creativity behind the bar – mind you, this was before the era of craft cocktails – and I wanted to keep learning.

Growing up, I learned how to cook for survival because I wanted to eat without spending a lot and I still wanted it to taste good. That introduced me to a lot of interesting food, a lot more than the beef, chicken, and pork I grew up with. My now-wife's family really inspired me, too. They're Eastern European so the food we'd have at their house was so different from what I'd grown up with and it made me realize how much possibility there is when it comes to what we can do with food.

I've always believed in using whole foods and trying to put the best thing on the plate that you possibly can. It's quality over quantity and, for some reason, that doesn't seem to be as common as I'd like it to be. For me, I've always stuck to my principles when it comes to what goes on the plate at Haven, but I sometimes I have to make sacrifices for budget and that's the reality of

"I think you can describe my food upbringing as a total Heinz 57 mix. I grew up eating a lot of tacos and my grandfather had a garden. He didn't really grow much, but I do remember we'd make sandwiches out of his icicle radishes."

"I am passionate about Grow Your Own. I put it off for a lot of my life, but it really is so simple and so rewarding, especially when you have kids.

I think, when you grow things or you know the people who grew them, you realize waste doesn't have to be wasted."

running a restaurant. I want to be doing things 100% right, 100% of the time, but sometimes I have to remind myself that it's about taking as many steps as possible in the right direction.

My experience with food was always pretty simple. Nothing was that wild but I loved the passion I'd see in people who had gardens. I remember the couple who lived across the street from me, they had this huge garden and during the summer I'd take care of it for a few months. My neighbor spent so much time building an irrigation system and talking to us about all the steps it took to grow these tomatoes and those cucumbers. They did a lot of preserving, too, so I got to see that. It's interesting, though, because they were from the Depression Era so, for them, growing food was much more, "This is just what you do and you have to do it."

I really believe in the possibility of not wasting food. In my kitchen, I try to look for solutions to the problem of waste: can we source direct from farmers, can we preserve something, can we use parts that might normally become waste? Using off-cuts, adding something to a dish... Have too many blackberries? Let's make blackberry beurre blanc. It's about thinking creatively and making a point to use what you have.

One of the reasons why more restaurants aren't changing their menu with the seasons, why they aren't sourcing locally, and all the rest is because it is more work. You have to have someone there who cares, otherwise it's a lot easier to do it the way it's been done in the past. Fortunately, I'm more than willing to do it.

I hope culinary schools start to have a more well-rounded and transparent discussion about how you can combine passion with business. There is value in caring about ingredients, changing your menu, and being progressive in the way you do things. Just because this is how it's always been done in restaurants doesn't mean that's how you have to do it.

For most kitchens, the hardest thing about sourcing is time. It takes so much time to source from a lot of different places and that's why a lot of chefs do it all through one vendor. At Haven, I started out with a ridiculous amount of vendors, trying to find the right point between quality and cost. Now we're focusing on just sourcing directly, working with local farmers and having them drop things off midweek so we can source more from them. It's working out really well, but it still takes time.

It's funny, but I want more home-growers and small farmers to just come knocking on my back door. I had a woman in Old Town Orange show up with a basket of tomatoes and I wanted to buy every single one. Licensed backyard growers can really change the game in terms of sourcing and I hope it becomes common practice. ❧

"I think the bottom line is: Do you care?"

"Growing food and sourcing food responsibly is empowering."

MONTH
July

CHEF
Greg Daniels, Haven Gastropub

FARMS
Local Backyard Farmers

This dinner truly began with the question: what ingredients do we have? Undeniably place-based, this meal was all about the height of summer and what fruit and veg had survived an early-season heatwave. Left with tomatoes and stone fruit, many of the dinner's ingredients were harvested from Evan Marks' homestead in Oceanside, California, The rest of the meal came from local farmers markets, including the Orange Farmers Market. It also sourced from social media and a handful of local backyard gardeners in and around Orange County.

"We cooked food we're really proud of tonight and when we go home, we know we supported good farmers and good people in our community."

— GREG DANIELS

ARRIVAL

Shiso taco

NEXT

Arugula and tomato salad with charred scallion and Meyer lemon vinaigrette

Compressed cantaloupe in basil syrup

Wild mushroom, egg, and grits

Crushed zucchini and black cod in sorrel broth

DESSERT

Yellow nectarine, honey, and vanilla-whipped sheep's yogurt

SHISO FISH TACOS

20 shiso leaves
1 tilapia fillet
1-2 sheets of kombu
2 avocados, sliced
1 cucumber, cut lengthwise, seeded and thinly sliced
1 Tbl chives, minced
4 oz tamari vinaigrette (recipe below)

2 oz tamari
2 oz rice wine vinegar
4 oz grape seed oil
1 shallot, minced
1 Tbl honey
- salt and pepper

FISH: Wrap the tilapia fillet in the kombu, and let cure for 1 hour. Slice into thin pieces.

TAMARI VINAIGRETTE: Whisk together all ingredients. While most of the seasoning comes from the tamari, you may season to taste with salt and pepper as well.

TACOS: Make your tacos by placing one of each on the shiso leaves: avocado, cucumber, tilapia. Dress with tamari vinaigrette and garnish with chives.

GOAT CHEESE GRITS

with wild mushrooms and sous-vide-poached egg

Serves 4-6

1 cup red flint polenta or grits
5 cups water
1 cup chèvre goat cheese
  - salt

4 cups assorted mushrooms
      for example:
      1 cup shiitake
      1 cup pioppino
      1 cup oyster
      1 cup crimini
  2 oz extra virgin olive oil
  2 oz butter
1 cup chicken stock
  - salt

  6 large eggs
  - water, as needed

GOAT CHEESE GRITS: Soak grits overnight in half of the water. Put in a heavy-bottomed saucepan, add remaining water, and bring to a simmer. Whisk throughout cooking process, which should be 45-60 minutes, until cooked through. Add more water to adjust consistency, if necessary. Add chèvre goat cheese and salt to taste.

WILD MUSHROOMS: Wash and trim mushrooms, removing any excess dirt or tough stems. Roast on a sheet tray in a preheated 400°F oven for 5-7 minutes to remove moisture. Sauté in a pan over medium heat in olive oil until tender. Add chicken stock, reducing by 75%. Stir in butter, and season with salt to taste.

SOUS-VIDE-POACHED EGG: Using an immersion circulator with a water bath, set to 143.3°F. Once it has reached temperature, lower your eggs into the water using a slotted spoon or spider. Wait for temperature to return, and cook for 75 minutes.

Eggs can be cooked up to 72 hours in advance and held refrigerated until needed. If choosing to do this, remove from hot water bath and place in an ice bath to chill for 10-15 minutes before refrigerating. When needed, prepare a water bath and circulator at 125°F and place eggs in the bath for about 5 minutes to warm through for service.

If using immediately, crack the egg into a small bowl containing a few ounces of warm water to clean away any watery egg whites. Use a spoon to gently remove the egg and serve.

CHARRED SCALLION AND MEYER LEMON VINAIGRETTE

over arugula and tomato salad

1 bunch scallions

2 Meyer lemons,
  zested and juiced

½ cup vinegar, preferably
  champagne or white wine

1 cup extra virgin olive oil

1 shallot, minced

1 clove garlic, minced

- salt and pepper

1 lb arugula

4-6 heirloom tomatoes

2-3 slices of brioche or
  sourdough bread

- olive oil

- salt and pepper

CHARRED SCALLION AND MEYER LEMON VINAIGRETTE: Heat a wide, heavy-bottomed saucepan (preferably cast iron) over high heat until smoking. Add scallions, turning to blacken evenly. Remove from pan, puree in blender, and set aside to cool. Whisk together with other ingredients. Salt and pepper to taste.

SALAD: Cut the slices of bread into ¼-inch cubes. Toss lightly in olive oil, salt and pepper. Bake in a 350°F oven until golden brown.

Cut the heirloom tomatoes into 2-3 bite size pieces. Mix with arugula, dress with the charred scallion and Meyer lemon vinaigrette, and season with salt and pepper. Top with croutons.

COMPRESSED CANTALOUPE IN BASIL SYRUP

1 cantaloupe,
  cut into 1-inch wedges

1 cup basil leaves, plus some
  reserved for garnish

1 cup water

1 cup sugar

Combine the basil, water, and sugar in a saucepot, and bring to a simmer, stirring occasionally, until the sugar is dissolved. Remove from heat, and allow to cool completely. Strain through a fine mesh sieve and set aside.

If you do not have a vacuum sealer, you can marinate the cantaloupe in the syrup for 3-4 hours under refrigeration. With a vacuum sealer, lay wedges on their side in the bag, add 2 oz of basil simple syrup, and seal under vacuum. The pressure will compress the fruit, and pull the syrup into it. This changes the texture and further accentuates the bright flavor of the fruit. Serve with fresh basil leaves.

BLACK COD WITH SORREL BROTH

and crushed zucchini

Serves 4-6

4-6   cod fillets
1 Tbl   extra virgin olive oil
1 Tbl   butter
  -    salt

2 cups   zucchini, quartered, core removed, diced into ½-inch squares
¾ cups   water
2 Tbl   extra virgin olive oil
2 Tbl   fresh picked thyme leaves
  3   cloves garlic, finely chopped
  -    salt and pepper

  3   bunches sorrel
  2   large shallots, sliced thinly
  2   cloves garlic, sliced thinly
1 pt   cream
1 pt   chicken stock
  -    salt

BLACK COD: Pat fish dry, and season both sides with salt. Use a large enough pan to not to be crowded when cooking. Place on high heat, and add one tablespoon olive oil, allowing to come to temperature. Add one tablespoon butter to the pan. Place the fish in the pan to sear, lower the heat to medium-high, and cook until it pulls away cleanly from the pan. Turn it over to barely cook the bottom side. Move to a "cooling" rack on a sheet tray and finish cooking in a 400°F oven until cooked through, about 4-6 minutes.

CRUSHED ZUCCHINI: Heat a wide, heavy-bottomed saucepan over high heat until almost smoking. Add olive oil to pan, and immediately add zucchini, thyme, and garlic. Stir constantly for 2 minutes, taking care not to brown the zucchini. Add water and cook over a high flame until all water has reduced and evaporated. Pour out on a sheet tray and refrigerate to cool. Pulse roughly in food processor. To serve, warm in a sauce pot and season with salt, pepper, and olive oil to taste.

SORREL BROTH: Blanch and shock two of the bunches of sorrel. Set aside.

Sweat shallots and garlic until translucent. Add remaining bunch of sorrel, and continue cooking until tender. Cover with chicken stock, bring to a simmer, and reduce by ½. Add cream and reduce by ¼. Season with salt to taste. Purée in a blender and strain through a fine mesh strainer. Chill.

Purée the blanched sorrel with enough cold water to blend. Mix with cooked purée before serving. Adjust seasoning if necessary.

TOMATO AND GOAT CHEESE TOAST

1	loaf pumpernickel, sliced
1 cup	goat cheese
4 oz	heavy cream
1	lemon, zested and juiced
1 pt	cherry tomatoes
2	yellow onions, thinly sliced
-	salt and pepper
4 Tbl	extra virgin olive oil
-	salt, preferably flake, to finish

Whip goat cheese in a mixer on medium speed, and slowly add the cream. Add lemon zest, a small amount of the juice, and season with salt and pepper. Set aside.

Heat 1-2 tablespoons of olive oil in a saucepan over medium heat. Add sliced onion and 1 teaspoon salt, stirring frequently and adjusting heat to prevent burning. It will take some time to bring out the caramelization from the natural sugars in the onion, about 30 minutes or more. Be patient, and your results will pay off. You want your onions to be sticky sweet and dark brown.

Blister the tomatoes in a hot cast iron pan, or roast them in a 450°F oven. Toast the pumpernickel, and cut into the serving size you would like (we like 2x4-inch pieces). Spread goat cheese from end to end, and top with caramelized onions and tomatoes. Drizzle with more olive oil and finish with a pinch of flake salt.

NECTARINES WITH HONEY AND VANILLA

on whipped sheep's milk yogurt

Serves: 4

4 nectarines, cut in half and pitted

- sugar

1 cup sheep's milk yogurt

1 Tbl honey

½ tsp vanilla paste or ½ vanilla bean, scraped

Whip the yogurt, honey, and vanilla in a mixer on medium speed.

Sprinkle each nectarine half with sugar, and roast in a preheated oven at 400°F until tender and just caramelized.

Add a smear of the yogurt mix to a small bowl or plate. Place half a peach and garnish with mint or basil.

CULTIVATE AND CONSUME A
DIVERSE VARIETY OF FOODS

Celebrate Diversity

Nature is abundant, it is diverse, and it
has more varieties than we can guess.
We need to grow and eat a diverse diet
full of different colors, textures, shapes,
and sizes; thus ensuring healthy bodies
and healthy soil.

Celebrate Diversity

EAT A VARIETY OF FOODS
AND EAT THEM OFTEN.

Every food has a unique nutritional profile so the more diversity we get in our diet, the more diverse and rounded our nutrition. The same goes for our soil: the greater variety of foods we grow, the richer and more regenerative our soil.

Nature provides us with the possibility of seemingly unending bounty but because of economics, efficiency and society's focus elsewhere, the variety of seeds we actively cultivate continues to narrow. Of course, part of this has to do with familiarity – growing the things we have always grown, buying the things we have always bought – but if we want to farm healthy soil, we must grow diversely. This not only means what we grow, but *how,* because the more dynamic our systems, the more diverse our foodshed and the closer to mimicking nature we become.

Conventional perennial farms, and even commercial organic farms, are too simplistic in their patterning. Diversity of crops is slim, with only annual row crops and a maximum of 12 varietals across a 26-acre field. It's not that we need hundreds of options on a small farm, but 12 crops are not enough for our diet. Unfortunately, most of the decision making around what is grown on a farm come from an economic standing. In other words: yield. As a result, more often than not, it's the less exciting and more conventional varietals that are planted because farms can plan on them. Growing risky crops may mean a greater yield, but it also means a higher potential for

"We don't want to see rows when we look out at farms, we want to see forests full of food."

lost dollars. They're looking for the safest, easiest to ship, highest yielding and, often, lowest flavor, with the most palatable texture.

Traditionally, farmers and gardeners were always seed savers. We would grow the varieties that grow best in our backyards and our farms, for our soils and our climate, and we grew foods that had the most nutrition, the most beautiful colors, that had the greatest textures, and had a diversity of harvesting times. Therefore, we would grow a variety of foods so that we could harvest throughout the season, with hyper-specific purposes for each.

Today, there are some leaders truly celebrating diversity, like the Baker Creek Seed Company. If you open up one of their catalogs, you can see thousands of things we simply are not growing. It's inspiring to see every variety of rainbow colored seeds, every shape and size, every vegetable. Seeing this reminds us how abundant agriculture can be, yet still we grow just a few things. Take, for example, Peru. Today, Peru is widely known for its quinoa, yet in *The Lost Crops of the Inca*, we are reminded how many unique food crops are in this one region, and Westerners know nothing about them. Over the last 15 years, quinoa has landed on

the culinary map when, previously, it was mainly only grown in the Andes, as it has been for potentially thousands of years. When it first came to the US market, it was a straw-colored grain, very predictable in that it fit in the color pattern with most other grains. But in the rural regions and agricultural communities of Peru, you can attend seed saving festivals where you'll see that this one seed we've come to know as straw-colored actually exists in every color of the rainbow: pink, purple, orange, green, red.

> "Eating a variety of foods is good for the environment, our diet, and the economy."

Simultaneously, there are so many other crops from that one part of the world that we have no idea about. We do know about the potato but we grow just a couple varieties of potato – the Russet primarily for french fries and others that have very little to no nutrition. We grow a couple other red and yellow potatoes, but there are actually over 2,000 varieties of potatoes and they all have a different color, shape, texture, nutritional value,

"Try buying a different type of vegetable each time you shop. So if you got a butternut squash last time, get an acorn squash this time, and a kabocha next time."

and climate. Depending on your elevation, your sun exposure, and a variety of other factors, you should be growing hyper-specific crops, not general crops.

Beyond potatoes, there are many other root crops that we don't know of – like the uyuco, oca, mashua, yacon – all these different types of tubers that have incredible economic opportunity but still live in the seed banks of the Andes.

We have barely begun to tap the potential of food diversity in the world and the variety and diversity of nutrition out there is mind-boggling. One of the only ways to really tap into it is to start growing our own.

It's inspiring to consider the wide variety of flavors ahead of us that we have never tried. Our gardens and farms can match the color of the rainbow and that's delicious. 🌱

Change it up.
Enjoy a variety of foods.

HOME

Grow heirloom varieties
of the more common fruit
and veg, saving seeds

Challenge your palette and
skills with one new ingredient each week or study
ingredients by region

Rotate your pantry
(drying your own spices
and herbs)

RESTAURANT

Highlight uncommon
ingredients, like heirloom
grains, exploring different
techniques and practices

Pick a staple ingredient
and find a different
(i.e. heirloom, more
uncommon) option

Make your own sour
bread, celebrating the
diversity of your local
bacteria

Makoto Chino

CHINO FAMILY FARMS;
RANCHO SANTA FE, CALIFORNIA

With a farm stand since 1952, Chino Family Farms has grown some of the most dynamic and varied produce California, and many restaurants, have ever had the chance to enjoy. Truly an inspiring operation, Chino Farms is crucial to the tradition of heirloom farming in California.

IN CONVERSATION WITH MAKOTO CHINO

My grandfather came to the States looking for his brother. He took a boat from Japan to Brazil and hiked up from Brazil to California, eventually finding his brother here. He got his farm in Oceanside, lost it during WWII, and then borrowed it back, one day paying off the loan, and that's where we are now.

All the family is involved. We each take our own part, with our own specialty. Wood cooks everything and takes care of the berries. AK used to do all the picking. We'll see what the next step is.

Without any brothers or sisters, the farm is really left to me and it's hard because there are a thousand things constantly in front of you. It's really one step at a time, hoping you don't fall down because you already don't have time to think about the future.

For us, we have so much biodiversity that we're in a state of constant research, learning new vegetables and how they grow. Trying to discover what the best seeds for old vegetables we have are, all while trying to be just a little bit better than yesterday.

We really have a passion for diversity here and I think that's been here from the start. We began with peppers and green beans, but a lot of different peppers, so we always had this penchant for things that were ethnically diverse. Of course we wanted to plant Asian vegetables because no one else was growing them

"What's our goal? To be 1% better every day. Have variety of one that's a little bit better. Know technology better, know whatever you can just a little better every single day. We have 50 different kinds of tomatoes. That's exhausting to think about every day. It's also amazing every day."

and we love that they aren't unique anymore. The fact that other people are growing them is a win, but it means we have to keep looking for the next thing we want to grow.

It's so much easier for people to grow things now. We used to smuggle seeds from France and Spain and Asian countries. It's a lot easier now, fortunately.

Growing in San Diego is pretty amazing for our diversity because we can have just about any climate we want. We can grow strawberries for 11-and-a-half months out of the year. Where else does that happen? You know, to be honest, I think we grow the best strawberry and even though it's really hard to find – it only lasts for about a day – they're so fragile and so special you can taste the variation each day, depending on water and temperature. It might be because I eat one every day so I can taste the difference, but still. I also love our corn. I can only eat it the day it's been picked though, because once the starch starts to break down, it tastes terrible to me.

"Alice Waters started buying from us back in 1971, when we shipped her some green beans and she realized this is what green beans are supposed to be like."

For us, we always want our vegetables to speak for us rather than us speak for us. We really go out of our way to respectfully and artfully harvest the food. We aren't big, but we take great care to be simple, to do it right.

I can't speak for the generations above me, but I feel like we earned a spot here by putting great pride into what we do. We were accepted through the vegetables we grow and we became part of the community, it's our identity. It's not just a job, this is who we are.

We save our seeds and while we do have heritage seeds, a lot are hybrids now so you only get one generation out of the plant. Unfortunately, America is about efficiency and shipping in food, not about variety. We have ten types of mustard, but people don't really even eat mustard greens so, to them, it's all just mustard. It's a journey of education that we have to take people on.

Even though we aren't a certified organic operation, you can trust us. We use crop rotation and we do everything we can because our customers are our community and we don't want to hurt our home.

Something I love that we grow and you can't really find are pea shoots. They're amazing, especially flowering pea shoots. They're great in salads because they have a little bit of texture, they aren't flat, so they hold up a dish. Fresh spinach raw. Radicchio, chicory, escarole – they're all so undervalued because of their bitterness, but just grill them with olive oil. I wish people wanted to make things like fava bean pesto instead of basil, using walnuts instead of pine nuts. I think it's really just about trying different but similar things.

In terms of diversity, seeking it is in everything we do. With about 60 types of tomatoes, ten types of beans, two types of strawberries, with three varieties in each; we also have a lot of squash and then even more we're testing. Really, I don't understand what the point is of growing the same thing every year. Why bother if you aren't trying your hardest? This work is far too difficult to wake up and do if you don't really care about it. Actually, it's impossible to be a farmer if you don't care, it's not just hard. I guess that's it: we care. 🌱

"It's an artful harvest.

It's our identity. It's not just a job, this is who we are. There's so much biodiversity not found in American supermarkets."

Ryan & Nikki Wilson

FIVE CROWNS;
CORONA DEL MAR, CALIFORNIA

Growing up in the Bay Area to a fourth-generation restaurant family, Ryan Wilson was raised with cooks. Everything was about the next meal and it simply was the how and why a day progressed. When Nikki and Ryan met, they fell in love over food, building a shared life around their work – she in pastry and he in the kitchen – and that's where they can be found today.

Discovering the interplay of food, travel, tradition, and culture with socialization and nourishment, Chefs Ryan and Nikki realized how integral the act of feeding one another is, and that's become their journey since.

IN CONVERSATION WITH CHEF RYAN WILSON

Even though I have English, German, and Scottish roots, our family is in love with Italian cooking. I've gotten to cook there a lot and since my wife is third-generation Sicilian, I think we at least have some roots.

Growing up, I was a very picky eater. I only ate shades of gray, nothing green, and I think it was a little bit youthful ignorance and a little bit arrogance. I just refused to try things unless it was exactly the way I wanted it. Eventually I studied abroad in Australia in college and realized that unless I wanted to eat ramen and pizza for the next few months, I'd have to start cooking. Fortunately, I'd grown up in a food family where we went to farmers markets every week and my mom had an incredible garden. So I just kept doing what I knew how to do and I found the markets. It's not easy, but I think you can source quality ingredients whether you're a small or large operation, it just takes time, passion, and dedication.

If you want to celebrate the seasons, you have to have someone at the helm of your restaurant willing to put the time and resources into finding what you want. You can't just read through an email of what's available from a vendor, it's actively going out and building relationships. It definitely is about knowing

"I love the controlled chaos of the kitchen. It all comes to a head at the table and the guest has no idea what happened behind those doors."

"It's not easy, but I think you can source quality ingredients whether you're a small or large operation, it just takes time, passion, and dedication."

what's at the market this week, but also about what's coming next week and that takes so much time and attention. Frankly, it's one of the hardest things to get a business to buy into. It takes a lot of extra hustle, and it's hard to manage, but when it works, it works.

I've been speaking to a rancher in Nebraska who has 100% organic Waygu-style beef and he sells directly to his clients. You can't find it through a distributor. Gems like that don't just happen. I've learned that you can't just go to the market, put it on your menu, and expect it to sell. You have to educate the front of house so they can let your customers know what's available. It's about inspiring them and getting them passionate about what you're excited about. Sometimes this is investing in some workshops, other times it's literally putting a garden in and having them get in there for some weeding. Those experiences translate into a powerful understanding about what we're doing on a larger scale. Chefs are driven to unique ingredients that spur creativity.

The diversity of an operation like Chino Farms is incredible. When I think about the seed saving they do to cultivate specific varieties, it's unbelievable. I think that if more chefs spoke to farmers like them, they'd understand what it's all about. Surprisingly, creativity doesn't come naturally for a lot of chefs, they have to really push for it. But I think with the right ingredients, creativity comes a lot easier.

IN CONVERSATION WITH NIKKI WILSON

I went to culinary school in San Francisco the first year Ryan and I were married because it's something I had always wanted to do. With Ryan's background, we put our heads together to figure out what made the most sense for me, and we decided on pastry. I love it, I love having the tools to know how to finish a meal and I think that's really what my responsibility is: how to appropriately finish a meal.

I love working with Ryan in the kitchen because it's a place we both aspire to retire to. He doesn't really get to be in the kitchen as much as he'd like and neither do I, so when we can, we just enjoy it. Our end product always seems to be better when we work together and it's just so... fun. It's fun to collaborate together.

The first meal he cooked for me was all from Chino Farms. Beautiful salad greens, hand-pressed pasta with local spot prawns and a light tomato broth sauce, this special rib eye, and wines from a trip to Italy he'd been saving.

From the food we eat to how we model our home, we try to bring their philosophy of diversity into our lives. We even ripped out our front lawn and the side yard so we could farm. Whenever we go down there, we always sneak a little inspiration from what they're growing.

I think it all really comes down to passion for us. When I had my previous career in finance, I used to dream about culinary school and then we made it a priority. We're really conscious of allocating our resources and time for each other so that we remain passionate about what we do, about food and hospitality. It's important to us and I just feel really grateful that we're in a spot where we can work together and have an influence. ❧

"I don't think there is anything more important than being able to provide organic, sustainable food. Supporting that agricultural system is essential."

May

Ryan & Nikki Wilson, Five Crowns

Chino Family Farms

Celebrating diversity is about celebrating our foodshed and eating some less-than-common things. And why not? Food should be a delicious adventure. Supporting farmers, bakers, fishermen, ranchers, winemakers, and everyone else involved in our foodshed gives them the chance to explore their craft, stewarding our landscape in a diverse and interesting way.

Most of our ingredients were sourced in a very left-of-center way, from paddleboard sardine pickups to backyard harvests, our chefs criss-crossed Southern California for the best (and most interesting) of the best.

"Ingredients can have many lives and this is part of cooking the natural way. The heart of seasonality is to not waste; it's to find uses for everything. One thing bleeds into the next, blurring hard lines so everything becomes a progression, offering the opportunity to not only think creatively, but also intelligently about how to use our resources."

– RYAN WILSON

FIRST

Tartine of local sardines on Prager Brothers rye with nasturtium sauce gribiche, radishes, and purslane

MAIN

Handmade cannelloni with first of season white corn, ricotta, and stinging nettle pesto

Roasted ronde de nice squash with California rice and Early Girl tomatoes

FINALLY

Golden beet genoise, strawberries, pistachios, creme fraiche, lemon verbena gelato, and borage flowers

OLIVE-OIL-CURED SARDINES

12	fresh sardines, 6-8 inches long, filleted and belly bones removed.
2 Tbl	fine red wine vinegar
2 Tbl	fine sea salt
2 Tbl	organic sugar
¼ tsp	fine ground chile d'arbol
¼ tsp	fine ground coriander
¼ tsp	fine ground black pepper
2 cups	extra virgin olive oil

A truly underappreciated (if not much maligned) Pacific fish, the sardine deserves a rejuvenation! While it is both delicious and nutritious, freshness is an absolute must, so look for plump 8-inch sardines with clear eyes and intact bellies. When these little guys get old, their eyes will turn red and the flesh around the belly will deteriorate. This is a great late-spring dish for brunch or lunch with a crisp white wine or rosé.

Line a sheet tray with parchment paper and lightly oil with extra virgin olive oil. Lay the sardine fillets skin side down on the parchment-lined sheet tray in one even layer. Brush the flesh side of the fillets lightly with the vinegar and reserve for 5-10 minutes to allow the vinegar to dry.

Mix the salt, sugar, chili, coriander, and black pepper in a small bowl. Season the fillets with the mixture and cover the tray with plastic wrap. Refrigerate for at least 6 hours, overnight if possible, but not longer than 12 hours.

After the fillets have cured, preheat an oven to as low as it will go, ideally between 160-180°F. Remove the plastic wrap and pour the olive oil over the fillets so that they are just covered.

Cook the sheet tray of sardine fillets in the oven for 30-40 minutes or until they have all but turned light gray and opaque. Remove from the oven and allow to cool to room temperature. The fillets can now be transferred to a clean flat bottom container. Cover with remaining olive oil and refrigerate until needed.

NASTURTIUM GRIBICHE

6	large eggs, hard boiled
1 Tbl	green garlic
1 tsp	lemon zest
1 Tbl	lemon juice
2 tsp	fine sea salt
½ tsp	freshly cracked pepper
2 Tbl	champagne vinegar
2 tsp	capers, finely chopped
2 cups	nasturtium leaves, packed
½ cup	parsley leaves
2 cups	extra virgin olive oil

Peel and rough chop the hard boiled eggs. Place in a large mixing bowl and reserve. Prepare and clean the green garlic by trimming the root end just above the roots and where the stem turns from light green to darker green.

Finely chop the green garlic and place in a medium bowl with the lemon zest, lemon juice, salt, pepper, champagne vinegar, and chopped capers. Allow to macerate for 15 minutes.

Meanwhile, clean and prepare the nasturtium leaves by removing the stems and washing them thoroughly, Be sure to harvest the leaves from an area that has not been sprayed with herbicide. Look for the smaller, more tender leaves.

Finely chop the nasturtium and parsley leaves and place in the blender with 1½ cups of olive oil. Blend on medium speed to incorporate.

Add 1 cup of the herb oil to the bowl of macerating green garlic. Taste for seasoning and balance of oil and acid. This dressing should have a brightness and sharpness to it without being overly pungent.

Serves 4-6

TARTINE ASSEMBLY

½ in	slices of course whole wheat or dark rye bread per person
-	tempered unsalted butter
-	lemon juice
-	extra virgin olive oil
-	flaked sea salt
-	nasturtium flowers to garnish
-	purslane
-	radish slices

To assemble the tartines, lightly toast the slices of bread under the broiler. Butter liberally from edge to edge and season lightly with some sea salt. Return the toasts to the broiler and toast again until the butter is bubbly and fragrant. Remove the toasts from the broiler and place on your cutting board.

Trim the toast of the crusts and cut in half, crosswise. Put the pieces back together and top with a liberal amount of the gribiche sauce. Place 3-4 cured sardine fillets on top of the gribiche and move the tartines to a plate.

Season lightly with sea salt, a few drops of lemon juice, and a generous drizzle of olive oil. Toss the purslane leaves and radish with a few drops of lemon juice, olive oil, and sea salt, and scatter on the plate around the tartines. Garnish with the nasturtium flowers and enjoy!

WHITE CORN CANNELLONI
with ricotta and stinging nettle pesto

This dish can be prepped a day advance and baked while your guests arrive.

Serves 4-6

5 cups	00 flour
1 tsp	sea salt
4	whole eggs
2	egg yolks
1 Tbl	extra virgin olive oil

8	ears of fresh white corn on the cob, shucked
4 Tbl	unsalted butter
1 Tbl	extra virgin olive oil
2 tsp	lemon juice
2 cups	cow's milk ricotta
½ cup	parmigiano reggiano, freshly grated
1 Tbl	sea salt
½ tsp	cracked black pepper

2 lbs	stinging nettles, picked and cleaned
¼ cup	walnuts, toasted
2	garlic cloves
1	tangerine, juice and zest separated
1 cup	extra virgin olive oil
1 Tbl	sea salt
½ tsp	cracked black pepper

PASTA: Mix together flour and salt in a large mixing bowl. Make a well in the middle of flour and add eggs, yolks, and olive oil. With a fork, beat together eggs and slowly incorporate flour until the dough starts to come together. Then, work the mixture together with a clean hand until the dough accepts as much of the flour as possible. There will be a natural and obvious point at which the dough has formed a mass. Discard the small amount of excess flour.

Dust a clean counter with flour and knead the dough for 7-10 min until the exterior has become slightly shiny and smooth yet springy to the touch. Wrap the dough in plastic and let rest for 30 min. Set up your pasta machine.

Cut ¼ of the dough from the ball. Flatten using hands so dough fits between rollers. Start on largest setting and roll the paste through, folding in half and repeating on the same setting twice. Repeat process for the first 3 settings. After third setting, dough does not need to be folded in half but roll the sheet through each setting twice, making the dough both thinner and more relaxed. Continue rolling out the dough until you have reached the second to last setting, when the sheet of pasta is thin enough to be just barely translucent.

Once rolled out, cut it to the length of a sheet tray and cover with a damp towel. Repeat the entire process for the remainder of the dough. Meanwhile, bring a pot of salted water to a boil and make an ice bath. Working in batches, blanch the sheets of pasta in the salted water for 2 minutes and remove to the ice bath to stop the cooking. Lay the blanched pasta sheets on a clean cutting board and trim to 4x4-inch squares. Now prepare the White Corn Filling and Stinging Nettle Pesto.

WHITE CORN AND RICOTTA FILLING: Grate only the flesh from 6 of the ears of corn into a large bowl. In a heavy bottom pot, heat 3 tablespoons of unsalted butter over medium heat. Add in the corn and 2 teaspoons salt. Stir and turn the heat down to medium-low. Cook slowly for 15-20 minutes until the corn cream begins to stiffen. Remove from the heat and pour into a clean mixing bowl.

Cut the kernels from the cob on the remaining 2 ears of corn. Sauté with 1 tablespoon of unsalted butter for 2 minutes, season with ½ teaspoon of salt,

Fresh pasta is unreasonably intimidating for the average cook. Give it a try a couple of times and you will quickly find that it's not only quick and easy but yields a truly superior and memorable dish. Plus, it's great fun to make with kids or for a date night!

then add to the cooked corn cream and remove from heat. Once cooled to room temperature, add ricotta, parmigiano, olive oil, lemon juice, additional salt and pepper to taste. Chill this stuffing for an hour.

Once chilled, the cannelloni is ready for assembly. Lay a 4x4-inch sheet of pasta on the counter and spoon a 1-inch diameter log of filling along one side. As tightly as possible, roll the pasta around the filling, making sure that the pasta sheet overlaps by approximately ¼-inch. Lift cannelloni off of the counter with a spatula and lay onto an oiled baking sheet. The cannelloni can be kept in the refrigerator overnight on the baking sheet.

STINGING NETTLE PESTO: Blanch the cleaned nettles in a large pot of boiling, salted water for 30 seconds and shock in the ice bath. Strain and wring out as much water as possible from the blanched nettles before chopping.

Add roughly chopped garlic cloves to food processor with walnuts, tangerine zest, ½ cup olive oil, and ½ of the salt and pepper. Pulse the mixture together to form a paste. Remove from food processor. Add chopped nettles to empty food processor with remainder of the olive oil and half of the tangerine juice. Add remainder of the salt and pepper and pulse for 30 seconds to combine and break nettles down more. Add the walnut mixture to the bowl and pulse to combine.

TO SERVE: Preheat oven to 400°F. Brush the top of the of the cannelloni with extra virgin olive oil and bake for 10 minutes until the edges of the pasta are golden brown and crispy. Plate the cannelloni with a spatula and top with the nettle pesto and a dusting of freshly grated parmigiano reggiano.

ROASTED RONDE DE NICE SQUASH

with California rice and Early Girl tomatoes

6	ronde de nice squash, tennis ball size
4 cups	cooked California rice
2 cups	farmer's cheese
½ cup	extra virgin olive oil
2 tsp	fresh lemon juice
½ tsp	cracked black pepper
½ cup	parmigiano reggiano
3 cups	cherry tomatoes, halved
1 Tbl	sea salt
4	cloves of garlic
2	bay leaves
2	whole chile de arbol
1 Tbl	sherry vinegar
2 cups	extra virgin olive oil
-	fresh basil

SQUASH AND RICE: Trim the tops off of the squash. The tops will be used for garnish. Using a small melon baller, carefully carve out the meat of the squash making sure to keep the walls of the squash consistently about ⅜-inch thick. Season the interior and the exterior of the squash with salt, brush with olive oil, and place upside down on an oiled baking sheet. Add the tops to the baking sheet as well. Pour 1 tablespoon of water into the baking sheet and bake the squash shells in a 350°F oven for 20-25 minutes until tender but not falling apart. Allow to cool to room temperature.

Chop the squash flesh to about the size of a kernel of rice. Heat a sauté pan over medium-high heat and add 1 tablespoon olive oil. Add the chopped squash meat and season with 1 teaspoon salt, sauté for 5 minutes to cook out some moisture and add a subtle color. Once cooked, pour the squash into a large mixing bowl.

Add cooked rice to the mixing bowl and add in farmer's cheese in small pieces. Season with salt, pepper, lemon juice, extra virgin olive oil, and the parmigiana cheese. Gently fold the mixture together, keeping some clumps of cheese intact. Stuff the par cooked squash shells with the rice mixture and reserve refrigerated for 1-2 days.

CHERRY TOMATO CONSERVA: Season the halved cherry tomatoes with sea salt and refrigerate for 2-3 hours at minimum, overnight is best.

Combine the seasoned cherry tomatoes, garlic cloves, bay leaves, chilies and vinegar with the olive oil in a shallow baking dish. Roast in a 225°F oven for 1½ hours. Remove from the oven and allow to cool slightly. Pour into a clean container and refrigerate until needed.

TO SERVE: Roast the stuffed squash in a preheated 350°F oven for 30-40 minutes. Warm the cherry tomatoes in a saucepan over low heat for 5 minutes.

Plate the hot stuffed squash and drizzle and garnish with the cherry tomato conserva. Grate fresh parmigiana cheese over the top and tear some basil leaves to garnish.

GOLDEN BEET GENOISE CAKE

1¼ cup	roasted beet puree
6½ cups	cake flour
7¼ cups	butter, melted
4	eggs
5 tsp	baking powder
6 tsp	vanilla extract
¼ cup	sugar
½ cup	rice vinegar
¼ cup	lemon juice
4 cups	milk

ROASTED BEET PUREE: Roast whole beets in oven at 400°F until tender. We like to coat them in extra virgin olive oil, add a thin layer of water to the roasting pan and cover pan with foil. Remove outer skin from roasted beets while warm and process insides in powerful blender until smooth.

CAKE: All wet ingredients should be brought to room temperature, including melted butter. Add all wet ingredients to a large mixing bowl. Sift dry ingredients over the bowl of wet ingredients and fold together with a whisk. Mix until cake batter comes together, careful to avoid clumps and overmixing. Pour batter into half sheet pan. Bake at 325°F until cake tester comes out clean.

LEMON VERBENA GELATO

2 cups	cream
2 cups	milk
1 cup	egg yolks
¾ cup	sugar
1 pint	lemon verbena leaves, loosely packed
-	berries or edible flowers, such as borage or calendula, as decoration

Set up an ice bath and have an instant-read thermometer available.

Combine half cream and half the milk in saucepot. Heat dairy mixture until simmering around the edges. Just before dairy is simmering, whisk together sugar and yolks in a bowl until a smooth ribbon consistency. Temper the yolk mixture with the dairy mixture by pouring a small amount of the warm dairy into the yolk mixture and then adding that back to the dairy on the stove. Anglaise, or cook to 180°F, being careful not to make scrambled eggs. Add remaining dairy to cool mixture, strain and cool in ice bath.

Add mixture to your ice cream maker and follow manufacturers instructions. Serve with Golden Beet Genoise Cake decorated with edible flowers.

MAKE FARMS
REGENERATIVE ECOSYSTEMS

Promote
Polycultures

Nature grows a lot of things all at once
and she doesn't do it in neat, tidy rows.
Polyculture farming, at its simplest, is
growing a variety of crops in imitation of
the diversity of our natural ecosystem. It is
the opposite of monoculture, or one crop,
farming. As one of the basic principles
of permaculture, polycultures include
tactics like multi-cropping, intercropping,
companion planting, beneficial weeds, and
alley cropping. Though it requires more
labor, polycultures prevent disease and
increase biodiversity.

Promote Polycultures

NATURE IS NOT A FACTORY.
NATURE IS DIVERSITY.

Ecosystems are inherently interconnected. With a variety of species, a diversity of harvesting times, and an abundance of annuals and perennials, a healthy ecosystem is constantly in movement. Polyculture farming seeks a dynamic balance where diversity breeds stability and resilience.

Nature is a regenerative ecosystem. It's hyper-dynamic, full of variety, and it craves diversity. Unfortunately, monoculture farming has fallen into favor with conventional agriculture because it is efficient,

predictable, and factory-like. With monoculture farming, farmers are able to grow one crop at scale. However, when a crop is grown at scale, the immune system of the earth is taxed, leaving the entire crop susceptible to pests, disease, and failure.

A lot of this has to do with the fact that conventional farming is actively working against nature. In direct contrast, polyculture farming is designed in imitation of nature and the natural ecosystem. Ideally, polyculture farming means food forests as opposed to the idea of a

for the animals and habitat for wildlife. Between the trees, there would be vegetables, herbs, and flowers; underneath, there are root vegetables.

This type of garden offers a beautiful, abundant assault to the senses that challenges the culture of farming. It offers the solution of farm as ecosystem, not factory, and it speaks to not only the health of the land, but the health of the individual. Economically, it must be considered that polyculture farming is more labor intensive than traditional monocropping. However, the end result in polyculture farming is a stronger, better crop with less waste, disease, and loss. Thus, with a dynamic harvest, farmers are able to come to market with a more robust offering for the community, full of a variety of fruits, vegetables, herbs, flowers, and animal products.

> ### "Mother Nature destroys monocultures."
>
> – MICHAEL POLLAN

"Monoculture farming" is defined as a high-yield agricultural practice on the same land, without rotation of other crops. It's often practiced with corn, soybeans, wheat, and even rice. In contrast, polyculture farming rotates crops and livestock to keep the land vital, meeting the complete nutritional needs of the local community while automatically replenishing the soil.

The most healthful diet one can consume is full of whole, fresh, locally grown food consumed in as close to its whole form as possible. The more variety in our diets, the better nourished our bodies will be. The same goes for the earth. When we tax the soil by only producing a single crop, it's as though we ate, one thing. Yes, on the surface monocrop farming is cheaper, but as Michael Pollan explains, "Cheap food is an illusion...The real cost of food is paid somewhere. And if it isn't paid at the cash register, it's charged to the environment or the public purse in the form of subsidies. And it's charged to your health."

Hyper-dynamic ecosystems are not the number of species that we're really talking about, it's the inter-

traditional farm, full of row crops. Instead, there should be a variety of plants and trees growing together, of all different shapes and sizes, full of vegetables and fruits and animals, working to steward the land. This approach is rooted in the idea of holistic management and has, until the modern era, really been the way farmers stewarded their land. Only once crops became commodities did polycultures become monocultures and did the regenerative health of the land came secondary to yield.

So what does a polyculture really look like? Ideally, the farmer harvests their own rainwater, rebuilding and restoring soil fertility on site through cover cropping, nitrogen fixating plants, animals, manure, and composting. They would implement a particular pattern of agriculture that allows for intercropping, or the planting of different crops together, like tree crops that not only produce fruit but provide food

"The main challenge with promoting polycultures over monoculture farming is that one must be committed to buying local, seasonal produce direct from the farmer. Otherwise, government subsidies will continue to push cheap food forward, strengthening the hold of very few on our food chain."

relationships we design for. It's the classic inter-crop polyculture that's timeless. A great example is corn, beans, and squash. We call it the Three Sisters and Americans throughout Latin and North America have been growing this polyculture forever. They wouldn't just grow corn on its own because it takes so many nutrients from the soil, but if you grow corn in partnership with beans, they replenish the soil through nitrogen fixation. By adding squash, you provide cover for the soil and that acts like a living mulch.

"As a farmer, you want to create healthy plants and healthy animals, all the way up the food chain. To do that, you make sure you create a soil that invites the right set of microbes. That's the job."

The best part of all this is not that it's just a perfect symbiosis with nature but that it's a symbiosis with culinary diet. That's a perfect protein, a perfect balance of nutrition; not just in the farm fields but in the kitchen. So it's taking that idea, that polyculture, that intercrop, and scaling it up. What does it look like to intercrop? What crops with what? In terms of fruits and vegetables, in terms of herbs and vegetables? That's when we start having fun because we're creating dynamic relationships and dynamic relationships eventually create ecological harmony as well as economic stability.

Polyculture farming, in practice, looks like alley cropping. This is where you have rows of fruit trees with rows of annual crops, allowing you to cultivate the soil of the farm every season.

With alley cropping, you can grow apples in a row, maybe even with five varietals in that row so you have an extended harvest, and between those apples you have mixed vegetables, providing great diversity for multiple harvests throughout the year. In addition, you may also have persimmons and any number of other crops, all extending your harvest.

Rebooting our relationship to agriculture means looking at it as an ecosystem that is diverse, dynamic, resilient, and abundant. Agriculture flows with nature, we can't forget that. ❧

Variety is key. Try new things and be curious.

HOME

Practice companion planting in your garden (like the Three Sisters)

Choose brewers who are using heirloom grains and are sending spent grains to farms

Talk to farmers about their growing practices; select biodynamic wines and the like

RESTAURANT

Work with farms who practice food forest techniques

Cook what farmers need to grow in order to grow healthy, resilient soil. Think of cover crops like fava, spelt, barley, and rye

Support aquaponics; a technique that grows vegetables and fish together

Alex Weiser

WEISER FAMILY FARMS;
TEHACHAPI, CALIFORNIA

Weiser Family Farms has been a family owned operation since 1977. As a second-generation farmer keen on continuing California's rich agricultural heritage, Alex's focus is on creating a biodiverse farm dedicated to applying sustainable farming techniques.

Alex Weiser's desire has always been to supply people with unique fruits and vegetables at their natural peak, not at their commercial yield peak. Today, Alex grows on 160 acres with that goal, farming in the greater Bakersfield area known as Tehachapi and the Lucerne Valley, cultivating a tapestry of high-quality produce year round.

IN CONVERSATION WITH ALEX WEISER

Our family farm started back in the 80s, when farmers markets were just getting going and, for me, that was perfect. I love the markets and it became such a joy to get to know my customers. It reinforces what I do because I know I'm connecting to people and contributing to their health with flavorful food.

On our land, we practice a theory known as polyculture farming. This is where you grow things that complement one another together, you rotate your crops in an intelligent way, you have good farming practices, and you really consider the soil. I think it's the best way to farm because it's, more or less, the closest we can get to how nature does it.

We also have tree crops, animals – kept on a separate ranch – and we don't waste any food. Protein isn't a big part of our business, but we like having options for ourselves, the chefs we work with, and our community. For us, we're looking at what it takes to make a good, healthy, and holistic farm system. Our theory is about always keeping the ground in use and to always be doing

"Every season has its crops for that time of year and, really, it seems like we're just using good old-fashioned farming practices."

something positive. That means we're either growing grain, cover crop, row crop, or a production crop.

One of my favorite things that we're committed to is the California Grain Project. In it, we're bringing back the old grains we used to grow. California has this great Mediterranean climate that is excellent for growing very high-quality grain. For some reason, grain as we know it is grown in the Midwest and it's not really because they grow it better there, but because their land is cheaper. They have a lot of land and a lot of rainfall, but their soil isn't what grain likes best. Grain likes really dry summers and rain in the fall and winter.

Up until the 1920s and 1930s, California was number two in grain production and then monoculture farming became common practice. Around that time, California shifted toward higher yield and more valuable crops and white flour

"It was only a hundred years ago that we stopped growing grain in California."

started to be grown where land was cheap. In resolution to that, our goal is to bring the grains we love back to the soil they thrive in.

Our lack of grain in California really comes down to a lack of infrastructure for small farms, especially in Southern California. So when chefs started to come to me asking for grain, I originally thought it would take thousands of acres to make it happen, fortunately it didn't and it still doesn't.

It's interesting because the demand for heirloom grains is actually what's made it possible for me to do what's better for the soil. Now that people want it, like heirloom tomatoes, it's worth it for me to harvest the grain I was already growing just for soil health. Having this huge diversity of grains to choose from, ones that all thrive here, that all have unique flavors, is exciting.

When we first started, we were producing grain in really small amounts and our customers loved it. The quality and flavor is what we kept hearing about. So we started to produce more, realizing there was a market for high-quality grains. Fortunately, this turned out to be a win-win for us because we're able to produce a crop that people want and it improves our soil. 🌱

"Even if I won the lottery, I'd still be a farmer. It gets in your blood."

Anna Maria Desipris

BEEKEEPER;
LAGUNA BEACH, CALIFORNIA

IN CONVERSATION WITH ANNA MARIA DESIPRIS

What makes bees so unique?

Bees are responsible for pollinating about a third of the food we eat. They're also considered a "super organism," meaning they operate cooperatively as one organism. So when the queen, male drones, and female workers come together, they work cohesively to achieve the goal of the hive. Bees are truly selfless creatures working for the good of the whole over the good of one.

Bees also create honey which is one of the oldest forms of medicine we have access to. This golden substance, which is a mixture of flower nectar and bee enzymes, can heal cuts, scrapes, wounds, and internal ailments. It can also be used to help alleviate seasonal allergies and hay fever. Such incredible medicine coming from tiny creatures, and the effort to create it – astounding! One honeybee creates a twelfth of a teaspoon of honey in her entire life. Interestingly, honey is also one of the oldest forms of currency in the world. It's been found in Egyptian tombs and many cultures have revered bees as a symbol of fertility, abundance, and divinity.

Honeybees love to live in and around cavities, like trees, which is where they were originally found. They use an internal mathematical equation that includes gravity, angle of the sun, their geographic location, and other factors to then come up with the right composition of wax that will hang and support the weight of the larva and honey inside.

What do you think we can learn from bees?

The health of our agricultural system and honeybee populations seemed to be stable until the late 1990s and early 2000s when we discovered a devastating collapse of honeybee populations. Huge losses in colonies since that time now happen every year, leaving commercial beekeepers with no stock, and farmers

"Honeybees are the most selfless animals. They work tirelessly, pollinating our food, and they do not do it for us, they do it for the success of their hive. We should operate as a hive."

"Bees are very fragile overall and they can't stand much more than what they've already endured."

with limited options for pollination. Since bees are an excellent indicator of the health of an ecosystem, it's clear that our system of monoculture farming, developed to feed the people of our nation, is actually crippling the environment and our honeybee population. By monocropping, we completely eradicate any concept of biodiversity. Until we can restore an environment with balanced ecology, multiple species and plants and organisms, the honeybee population will continue to decline.

The conversation around honeybees is actually a conversation around our food system. Honeybees are at once the symbol of what we're doing wrong but they're also showing us what we can do right. They're showing us their incredible perseverance and ability to adapt in a quick amount of time. They are relentless and will continue to try to survive despite the conditions we are putting them through, but they cannot do it forever. They have unbelievable resilience but they cannot win this battle without effort on our part.

I think the most important thing we can do at the individual level to help bees is to create ecosystems and healthy habitats. As we expand in the urban environment, we take away from the bees' potential habitat. This means we have to consciously make up for it. Bees need plants so they can forage and feed themselves. Consider planting a pollinator garden and plant in blocks, like a patch of rosemary next to a patch of lavender so it is more efficient for the bees when they harvest. Finally, always call a beekeeper to save a hive rather than an exterminator. Every hive deserves to be saved and relocated to a safe place to thrive. 🌱

Rich Mead

FARMHOUSE AT ROGER'S GARDENS; NEWPORT BEACH, CALIFORNIA

From dish washing to cooking, Chef Rich Mead has worked in kitchens nearly his entire life, handling just about every job there is. Focused on craft and ingredients, he bridges the gap between back of house and front of the house with a savvy sense of business, charm, and commitment to the food.

For a chef like Rich Mead, promoting polycultures is really about letting the ingredients and farmers dictate his sourcing. By asking for variety and buying it, he gives farmers a reason to grow unexpected crops, thus benefiting their ecosystems and his menu.

IN CONVERSATION WITH CHEF RICH MEAD

Having a background in economics, I've always thought about food as a really interesting give and take between farmer and chef, restaurant and guest. In 1983, we opened our first restaurant in Sherman Oaks called Stanley's and those first five years were a crash course. I got immersed in the food scene and made a lot of friends, from the people growing food to catching the fish and making the food. It's funny, even back then, I'd get calls in the middle of the night from my friends who had just been out on the boat, pulling in fresh tuna and asking if I wanted to buy it. Of course I did. These were the guys I'd sit around with, filleting 200 lbs of albacore with, talking about opening restaurants with.

After five years, I went to La Cienega, eventually opening Seventeenth Street Café in 1992 as the chef. Pretty quickly I learned that in order to do the things we wanted, we had to raise money. We started with two diners, then twelve, and eventually we got enough customers who liked what we were doing and that's when we started to go to farmers markets.

The biggest thing I ever learned, though, was that if you got produce from a produce company, you always got the same thing, but if you went to the market, you started to have parameters put on you about what you could cook. Not

"I think it's essential to educate young people, especially in culinary school, about where produce comes from. It should come from a farm, not a produce company. You should have to wash it when it comes in. This immediacy makes it exciting."

"When I learn how the farmers grow the produce I use, I can tell their story to my chefs and the front of house, they tell it to the customer and we all get educated. It starts with convincing them that what we're doing is good and necessary, though. That's not hard when it tastes this good."

everything was always available and the question suddenly became, what could you make with what was at hand?

Working with what was available gave us a reason to develop new ideas. We'd go to the market and then come back and try to figure out a tasting menu for sage. Eventually, I made a commitment to only using produce from the market, trying different purveyors, and genuinely building relationships with the people we were working with.

The best part in those early years was the conversation around what other people were doing, collaborating on how you did it and how I did it. We wanted to help each other figure it out.

Eventually, after a few restaurants, we started doing a few farm dinners, then a few more. For me, showing people where their food comes from was so important. I wanted people to see that farmers are artisans and they're the ones who give me the raw materials to do what I do.

In terms of diversity, I think when chefs choose to source directly from farmers, we're giving them the sense of security they need to plant more diverse crops. This diversity actually really benefits us because the more diverse the crops are, the better the soil becomes. 🌱

"Chefs have to be leaders in our community. We have to do everything we can to make education accessible."

MONTH # October

CHEF # Rich Mead, Farmhouse at Roger's Garden

FARM # Weiser Family Farms

Tasked with embodying the spirit of "Full Circle," this meal asked how we can make farms not just sustainable, but regenerative ecosystems.

Held in the middle of October, this dinner embodied the season's full shift to fall. With stone fruits and tomatoes gone, the meal was really about hearty grains and savory flavors from the smoky cob oven. Think about Tehachapi Apple Bread Pudding and all those autumnal notes.

"First we eat, then we do everything else."

– MFK FISHER

MENU

Vietnamese pork meatball lettuce wraps with rice noodles and sweet chile sauce

Roast carrots, burrata cheese, extra virgin olive oil

Guajillo, tomatillo, and beer-braised heritage pork with pee wee potatoes and braised Bermuda onions
+ slow cooked collard greens and caramelized onions

DESSERT

Brioche Tehachapi apple bread pudding in mini pumpkins

VIETNAMESE-STYLE PORK MEATBALLS
in lettuce wraps

Serves 4-6

1½ lbs   full-fat ground pork

2½ Tbl   fish sauce

1¼ tsp   fresh ground black pepper

4   shallots, minced

4 tsp   sugar

½ cup   peanut oil

12 oz   dried rice noodles

3 qts   water

1   medium butter leaf lettuce head, washed, patted dry, and separated

2½ Tbl   sugar

¼ cup   water

¼ cup   distilled white vinegar

2   garlic cloves, minced

1 Tbl   chili paste

-   salt to taste

2 Tbl   lemongrass, minced

½   yellow onion, minced

1   jalapeño, minced

1   friggitello pepper, minced

1 Tbl   garlic, minced

¼ cup   white wine

3 Tbl   pickling liquid

2 Tbl   fish sauce

MEATBALLS: In a medium bowl, mix together first five ingredients, and refrigerate overnight, about 8-24 hours.

In a medium pot, bring water to a boil. Add rice noodles and stir to separate. Cook for about 2-3 minutes or until noodles are al dente. Drain and rinse well. (If noodles begin to stick, toss in a little peanut oil.) Toss with Thai sweet and spicy sauce (recipe below). Set aside.

Heat oven to 325°F. While noodles are resting, begin to form gumball size meatballs. Once formed, heat a medium size frying pan on medium-high, and add oil. Working in batches, brown meatballs on all sides. Place on a sheet tray. Bake meatballs for about 15-20 minutes or until juices run clear. Set aside.

THAI SWEET AND SPICY SAUCE: In a medium bowl, mix together sugar, water, white vinegar, minced garlic, and chili paste. Heat a saucepan on medium-high. Once hot, reduce to medium and add ingredients from the bowl. Allow to simmer on low heat until sauce begins to thicken. Add salt to taste. Remove from heat, and allow to cool 2-3 hours or overnight.

LEMONGRASS CHILE RELISH: Combine all ingredients in a small bowl. Adjust relish according to taste preferences.

TO PLATE: Place rice noodles inside lettuce leaves, then top with meatballs and lemongrass relish. Enjoy!

ROASTED CARROTS & TOPS WITH BURRATA

Serves 4-6

1½ lb   small carrots with tops, washed

½ cup   extra virgin olive oil

  -   salt and pepper

  3   garlic cloves, chopped

¼ tsp   crushed chili flakes

2 Tbl   lemon juice

2 Tbl   white wine

½ lb   burrata

Preheat oven to 350°F.

Remove carrot tops and set aside. Toss the carrots with ¼ cup of olive oil, salt, and freshly ground pepper, place on a sheet pan covered with parchment paper and put in oven for about 30 minutes or until soft to touch. Remove from oven and set aside.

Clean tops by blanching in salted, boiling water. Dry well and place in a food processor with chopped garlic, crushed chile, lemon juice, and white wine. Salt and pepper to taste. While pureeing, drizzle in the other ¼ cup of extra virgin olive oil until you reach a consistency of a loose paste or pesto.

TO PLATE: Cut burrata in halves and place asymmetrically on a platter. Pile on baked carrots and drizzle with carrot top pesto and extra virgin olive oil. Salt and pepper to taste.

BRAISED COLLARD GREENS

with tongue of fire beans

1 tsp	olive oil
2	medium onions, julienned
2	garlic cloves, chopped
1 Tbl	crushed red chili flakes
2 lbs	collard greens, cleaned, de-stemmed, and chopped
¼ cup	white wine
1½ cup	vegetable stock
-	salt and pepper
1½ Tbl	apple cider vinegar
1½ cup	dried tongue of fire or borlotti (cranberry) beans
-	cooking liquid or broth for beans

Heat a large skillet on high, once hot reduce to medium, add oil and sauté onions with crushed red chili flakes. Add chopped garlic on top of onion, offering a buffer from direct heat, to keep from burning. Next, add collard greens, and stir until they begin to wilt. Add white wine and reduce by ½.

Reduce heat to medium-low and add vegetable stock, and salt and pepper to taste, and allow to simmer until greens begin to soften, about 5-7 minutes.

Cook until the greens are tender and most of the liquid is evaporated, about 5-10 minutes. Just before serving, add apple cider vinegar.

Cook the beans separate in seasoned water until tender and let them cool in their cooking liquid. Stir carefully into collard greens last.

NOTE: You could use chicken stock or water and ham hocks or some type of smoked pork in this.

TO PLATE: See recipes on following spread. Slice and place pork on top of collard greens and beans in pan with pureed braising liquid. Place potatoes and onions around the pork and greens.

HERITAGE PORK SHOULDER

braised with tomatillo, beer, and guajillo chili

Serves 4-6

1 Tbl	salt
½ tsp	fresh ground pepper
¾ tsp	chili powder
1	pinch cayenne
½ tsp	garlic powder
½ tsp	onion powder
½ tsp	ground cumin
½ tsp	paprika
3 lb	boneless pork shoulder
2 Tbl	peanut oil
2	bottles dark beer
1 lb	tomatillos, husked
3	garlic cloves
2	yellow onions
3	guajillo chilies, toasted without seeds
1	jalapeño
2	friggitello chilies
1	small bundle fresh thyme
3	rosemary branches
3	bay leaves
1	orange, zested
1	lime, zested

Preheat oven to 325°F. In a small mixing bowl, combine the first eight ingredients to create a dry rub. Thoroughly rub pork with spice rub, and allow to sit for a few hours, until it reaches room temperature.

Heat a large cast iron or heavy-bottomed pan on high. Once hot, reduce to medium-high and add peanut oil. Sear pork in the pan on all sides, to give the shoulder some color, about 3 minutes on each side. Once seared, tie thyme and rosemary into a small bundle with food-safe twine. Place pork and bundle in a roasting pan with vegetables, chilies, herbs, zest and beer. Cook until roast is tender and is easy to pierce with a large fork, about 45 minutes to an hour.

Place pork on a tray and cover, then allow to cool for about an hour before placing in the refrigerator to cool overnight. Place braising liquid in a container and chill in refrigerator.

When ready to serve, skim fat off the top of liquid and remove bay leaves, thyme, and rosemary. Puree in blender and add salt and pepper to taste. You will use this liquid to reheat your pork.

NOTE: You can roast the pork and onions simultaneously.

BRAISED CANDIED ONIONS

3	medium onions
-	salt and pepper
3 Tbl	extra virgin olive oil
2	rosemary sprigs
¼ cup	white wine

Preheat oven to 350°F.

Heat a large oven-safe sauté pan on high. Once hot, reduce to medium and sauté onions in a pan with salt, pepper, rosemary sprigs, and oil. Deglaze the pan with white wine and place in the oven. Roast until caramelized, about 15-20 minutes.

ROASTED PEEWEE POTATOES

3 lbs peewee potatoes, washed
  - salt and pepper
3 Tbl olive oil

In a large pot, place potatoes with cold water and bring to a simmer. Cook until just done, about 10 minutes, drain and toss with salt.

Preheat oven to 450°F.

About 15 minutes before serving, toss the potatoes with olive oil, salt and pepper to taste, and place uncovered on a baking tray in oven. Stir occasionally until potatoes brown a bit.

BRIOCHE TEHACHAPI APPLE BREAD PUDDING

2 cups	brioche bread, cut into ½-inch cubes
1	large or 2 small granny smith apples, or tart apple of your choice, diced very finely
2 Tbl	butter
¼ tsp	ground cinnamon
¼ tsp	ground clove
¼ tsp	ground cardamom
1 ¼ cup	heavy cream
1	whole egg
1	yolk
¼ cup	brown sugar
½ tsp	vanilla extract

Preheat oven to 350°F.

Lay cut bread pieces on a sheet tray and toast for 5-8 minutes or until just lightly crisped at the edges. Remove from oven and set aside.

Heat a pan on medium and once hot, add butter, apple pieces, and spices. Toss in pan for 1-2 minutes until combined and slightly softened.

In a separate pan, warm the cream over medium-low heat until the slightest simmer. Do not boil. Remove from heat.

In a separate bowl, whisk together the egg, yolk, and brown sugar. Slowly stream in the warm cream, whisking the entire time to combine.

Grease (I use butter) an oven-safe dish/pan, add bread and apple mixture and stir. Then pour over the custard mixture and stir again. Let sit/soak for 25 minutes, and then bake for 25 minutes or until toothpick comes out clean.

NOTES: For this recipe, I was lucky enough to have my friends at BREAD Artisan Bakery make brioche loaves for me with Alex Weiser's freshly milled Sonora wheat. Those loaves were such a beautiful start to the dessert. I was able to get some of his mini pumpkins and decided that was a great way to plate and share this dessert. Although I didn't cook the bread pudding in the pumpkins, that would be a great option if you used a tasty small edible pumpkin or squash. Top with freshly whipped cream or serve with ice cream.

GIVE CHILDREN EVERYWHERE ACCESS
TO DELICIOUS, HEALTHY FOOD

Nourish
all Children

We can build a hopeful future, but we have to start today and step one is access. It's caring for our children by creating non-negotiable standards of accessibility for all.

Nourish All Children

EVERY PERSON, EVERY CHILD, AND
EVERY ANIMAL SHOULD BE CARED FOR

Access and education should not be a limiting factor and nothing should prevent our children from growing up with healthy, nutritious food, understanding that we are part of our food system, that we are responsible for our future, and that we have the ability to create beautiful, thriving ecosystems that take care of us.

A truly holistic path to stewardship depends on our ability to love all children, of all species, for all time. The ultimate, tangible application of this principle is for all schools to serve delicious, nutritious, organic food every day, for free, in their cafeteria. An organic salad bar is great, access to a school garden is phenomenal, but when schools are still serving processed foods with zero nutrition, we're limiting the potential of our children.

Of course, all the principles are interconnected, but to "Nourish All Children," we have to see how intimately tied it is to eating fresh and how that ties back to buying local and seasonal; in turn, seasonality supports

polycultures, and so on. This all comes back to regeneration and, for us, we believe a regenerative future is embodied by our children.

We have a responsibility to nourish all children, their hearts, their minds, and their stomachs. There's great humanity in the natural world and children, unarguably, are beautiful and sacred. To nourish all children allows us to do our duty as humans because everyone, everywhere, should have access to healthy, nutritious, delicious, local food. This very concept is what re-engages farmers and communities in the conversation of food.

Not that long ago, all food was local. We grew locally for our communities and we grew food everywhere – backyard gardens, fruit trees – and farmers were prevalent. Just like we had a local hardware store, local doctor, and local pharmacist, we had a local farmer and a local source of produce. These were the basic building blocks of a healthy community. Only once agriculture became industrialized and the idea that all types of food should be available everywhere, all the time, did

we start to replace local agriculture with industrial dependency. In the name of ease we lost our integrity, and the environment and our bodies have suffered for it. Nourishment and food have to come from our local soil, it cannot be flown in from thousands of miles away.

The question is, what would it look like for our children to be nourished? How would their brains function at a higher capacity? What would their creativity look like? What would the community around us need to be to support the idea that our children are important and that food is what sustains us?

> "Nourishment is the key to health and health is obviously the key to living a happy life."

Ideally, we're measuring the success of our humans based on their happiness and, ultimately, based on their health. For us, "health" and "happiness" are interchangeable. It all comes back to how we eat and how we see ourselves on the planet. Starting with food, it's essential that we reconnect with the environment around us.

Alice Waters has been working on the idea of nourishing all children for at least 30 years. She's modeled this with schools in Berkeley, where they've built an edible schoolyard, integrated edible education into the classrooms, and all students are eating food from the garden while also learning how to make it. This is incredibly inspiring and we need to get more kids with their hands in the soil, learning how to prepare culturally unique, colorful, seasonal meals.

The truth is, you can teach every lesson in the garden and you can teach every subject in the kitchen. There's no reason why we have to stay walled in, and it's our hope to start teaching chemistry through baking and history through the food on a plate.

Nourishing all children is about connecting real food to our schools and home. 🌱

Access to healthy, nourishing food should never be an issue.

HOME

Take steps to eliminate preservative laden food from your pantry

Eat a meal together, cook together, prep and buy food together

Teach your children (or nieces and nephews) a traditional skill or family dish

RESTAURANT

Sponsor a school garden and help to cater fundraisers for community gardening programs

Support a salad bar in a school by helping to get one started in a school near you

Host a cooking class for families. Try fun menus such as flatbreads topped with seasonal veggies and homemade pizza

Holly Carpenter

THE GROWING EXPERIENCE;
NORTH LONG BEACH, LOS ANGELES

The Growing Experience is a seven-acre urban farm located in north Long Beach, California. They have four acres of farmland and three acres of dedicated community garden with a community events space.

This land is a unique model for urban farming in that it is owned and operated by Los Angeles County and the housing authority.

IN CONVERSATION WITH HOLLY CARPENTER

We're focused on providing access to food for people who are traditionally underserved. North Long Beach is known as a food desert – meaning there is not a lot of access to fresh food. Many grocery stores are prohibitively far away for residents or if you can get to a store, it might not have any organic or even fresh produce available.

Our primary method of distribution is our CSA program where we provide a veggie box full of eight to ten seasonal fruits and vegetables to folks who are investing in the farm. We also have a weekly farm stand for residents to access fresh food.

We also seek to promote the local food system and local economy by providing limited sale to restaurants, juice bars, and chefs like Chef Paul Buchanan. We want to expand the reach that our produce has. We're a community farm. We aren't for profit and we aren't looking to make money. Our programs are focused on outreach, education, and community.

We want to become a food hub that can produce local goods at scale. So local jams, honeys, and the like to people who wouldn't otherwise have access. Something we're really proud of is introducing fresh fruits and vegetables to the local preschool, developing a permaculture food forest with drought tolerant plants. We also have an at-risk youth program with the local schools where we

"The work we do helps people who want to be part of a healthier life but their circumstances have left them disenfranchised from that."

"It's important to look at sourcing and consuming local food as a discipline."

bring students to the farm, having them get their hands dirty, learning about nutrition, and going on field trips. This helps them keep their time occupied in a positive way. We also have a large-scale aquaponics system that helps us research different solutions for growing in an urban setting.

Expanding our knowledge around growing methods allows us to convert a parking lot or a rooftop into a productive area. Our goal is to expose youth from our community to growing methods and skills they can use throughout their life. Different events we hold for the community throughout the year let us introduce growing food as an accessible activity for our residents. Really, our whole goal is to get people involved.

On the farm, there is always work to do because you can't just plant one thing and be done with it. There's a cycle. There's also a lot of untapped potential on our land and the more we get people in, the more we have helping hands, the more we can get done.

With labor, our four acres could supply a large percentage of the vegetables for farm-to-table restaurants in Long Beach. This land can produce a lot, but we need help. If we could grow more, our reach and impact would potentially even benefit the local school system. It's really about our ability to produce at scale and that comes down to labor right now.

We can get a lot done with volunteers, but to get the daily work of weeding, harvesting, propagating, and the like done, you need continual labor.

Right now, we need to push for education in non-affluent communities and to get access to people who do not have access. Of course, we have to be sensitive, but we also have to provide the tools and the education for people to grow their own food in a way that is affordable. In the long run, it's urban farms like ours that will help turn food deserts into food forests. 🌿

Paul Buchanan

PRIMAL ALCHEMY;
LONG BEACH, CALIFORNIA

Chef Paul Buchanan has been a fixture of the Southern California slow food scene since the beginning. With years of experience, Chef Paul has an unerring dedication to his craft, fostering meaningful relationships with growers and community organizations alike. As a champion for accessibility to good food, farm-to-table has been his touchstone from the start.

Always looking for ways to waste less and do better, Chef Paul built a charcuterie cabinet in his home kitchen, curing meat, smoking bacon, and breaking his own whole pigs with the intention of using every part. As a Master Preserver, it's easy to see what he's curious about as a chef, whether it's now or months prior, his menus speak of jams, pickles, charcuterie, and larder goods he can add to a dish, no matter the season.

Committed to local fare, Chef Paul supports farmers and purveyors who do things the right way. To him, "the right way" means paying attention to details, providing the thoughtful, well-rounded ingredients that finish a meal. Balanced without pushing tradition, Chef Paul's food really speaks through his mastered skill set.

As a thought leader in his community, Chef Paul is devoted to mentorship, education, schoolyard gardens, and advocacy for policy change. It is a family affair as well with his wife as his business partner and his teenage daughter helping in the kitchen and on events.

IN CONVERSATION WITH CHEF PAUL BUCHANAN

Primal Alchemy Catering is something that came about after I had worked in a lot of restaurants. I had worked for a variety of other chefs and realized I wanted to take on my own style. Since I always loved to grow my own vegetables, whenever I could, I wanted to bring that fresh taste to my catering clients.

I often get asked why I cater rather than running my own restaurant and I think the easiest way to explain it is that I have a teenage daughter who knows who I

"Thoughtful and whimsical with a story of sustainability."

"I want people to want the apple with a wormhole. That means it was good enough for a worm to want it."

am. Just as much as I care about the food I make and the farmers I work with, I make a point to share food and time with my family. Connecting over the table is what it's all about for us. It's such a bonding experience.

Our perception of food has been so skewed and it's mostly because of media, advertising, and the marketing dollar. People think they want the perfect apple, but that's just because they don't know that apple has been bred for shelf life, not flavor, and then there's the paraffin coating...

> **"I am fascinated by the alchemy of food. I want to know what happens when you add vinegar, how to make something bitter, sweet, sour, spicy. I want to know what happens on a primal level to make that bite perfect."**

To me, places like The Growing Experience, Farm Lot 59, and urban farms in general are essential. These small farms show us you can grow food wherever there's space. You don't need a perfect farm, you just need a place to grow; and it's this sort of entrepreneurial spirit that can help us eradicate food deserts in our communities. Again, it's really all about access and how-to knowledge. In addition, I love to see farmers markets becoming the norm, rather than the exception, now.

I think that if you follow the insects, the worms and the birds, you're going to find what's good to eat. I genuinely think we should be learning from them.

I get so excited about seasonal produce. It's an amazing thing because the produce tells you when it's at its best. So, for squashes and gourds, we grow them all summer long and into the fall; and then, the stem gets hard and dries up. That's the moment when pumpkins convert their starches into sugars and that pumpkin will taste its best. It's phenomenal – if you were to eat a pumpkin the day you picked it, it would be starchy. If you're patient and wait like it wants you to, it'll be as sweet as pie. The opposite is true for corn; the day you pick it is ultimately the sweetest it will ever be, the longer you wait, the starchier it becomes. This is the cool thing about food, the science that makes me want to keep learning more and more.

> **"I have always loved farm-to-table, way before it was a thing. For me, it was because there was something nearby, though – it's because I had access to it"**

It all comes down to education. I've spent over 18 years educating kids that they want the orange that fell off the neighbor's tree more than they want the one in the grocery store. I love sharing the extra cucumbers I grow because when my neighbors grow too much of something else, they're going to share with me. That's the whole point of food and community and caring for one another.

I think that if we start to shift our perspective, we'll see a lot of possibility around us. For example, in Long Beach, there is a lot of fallen fruit. Some of it gets collected and donated to the homeless, but what about the rest? I love taking that excess and making it into jams and jellies, harvesting from the urban orchard and turning what would have been waste into something meaningful and delicious. To me, that's the challenge of it all: how can we be creative and rethink what it means to fully use our resources?

Looking back, skills that used to be second nature to people are starting to be prevalent again today. Things like preservation techniques, farming animals, butchery, being tuned into harvest time of seasonal foods, and the like. These are skills we need to actively pursue, we can't just assume the knowledge is going to stay with us if we don't use it.

I think part of the process is putting yourself in the way of learning. For me, I will never know everything about food, I attend a lot of educational gatherings and am always curious about all things food. I make it a choice to feed my family and my clients good food. Education around food is education about economy and that knowledge is power. We shouldn't be afraid to give our kids the power of knowledge.

We need to know how to treat food. The same way wolves teach the young how to hunt, we must teach our kids how to know what is good for them. We have to fight the battle of the large food commodities that market to our kids if we are going to win the war for real food. ❧

"I want to see people turn their lots into gardens. Let's use open space. I'd much rather see gardens than abandoned lots."

MONTH

January

CHEF

Paul Buchanan, Primal Alchemy

FARM

The Growing Experience

Influenced by the natural intelligence and alchemy of food, Chef Paul Buchanan is an expert and forever-student of the time-tested skills and methods people have always used when preparing and preserving the harvest. Amazed by the beauty of imperfect produce, Chef Paul's dinner connected the familiarity of traditional cuisine with the unexpected flavors and practices of heirloom homestead ways. Weaving ingredients between courses, this meal was a nod to the season as well as the preservation of seasons past.

"Harold McGee called cooking the 'Primal Alchemy,' the first science man ever practiced. We changed food by cooking it because it tasted better. We turn it into gold."

– PAUL BUCHANAN

APPETIZERS

Snap peas with house-made goat milk ricotta and pickled onion relish

Santa Barbara abalone ceviche with Lim's Farm cucumber, shaved radish, and sesame

MAINS

Jasmine flower borscht soup with sour cream beside butternut squash soup with maple whipped cream

Lemongrass marinated roasted rockfish with farro risotto, Castilla pumpkin, and braised greens

DESSERT

Port-poached Lim's Farm bosc pear tart with raw, dried California macadamia nuts

GOAT MILK RICOTTA CHEESE

1 gallon   goat milk (unpasteurized is ideal, but not required)
1 tsp   citric acid or lemon juice

In a stainless steel pot, heat the milk to exactly 180°F, using a thermometer. Remove from heat and stir in the citric acid (or lemon juice). Cover and allow to sit for at least 10 minutes. Stir to separate the curds and whey. (If the milk doesn't look like it has separated, you can add pinches of citric acid or lemon juice until the separation starts, but remember: A little goes a long way!)

Set up a fine mesh strainer with cheesecloth inside to catch the curds. Pour the cheese mixture over the cheesecloth, with a bowl or container to catch the whey underneath. Allow the strainer to sit over the container and chill for an hour or two. Pull the cheesecloth out of the strainer, mindful of the curds inside and transfer the ricotta into another bowl.

Season the ricotta with salt to taste. You can flavor the cheese in whatever ways you like, be creative!

TIP: If the curds have become too dry in the hanging process, you can incorporate some of the whey back into the ricotta to make it creamier. The whey can be saved and used in a number of ways, including as a vinaigrette for salads!

PICKLED ONIONS

5   large red onions
1 cup   white wine or apple cider vinegar
2 cups   sugar
3 cups   water
5-10   peppercorns (black, white, or medley will all work)
2-3   bay leaves
  -    pinch of chili flakes
5-8   allspice berries
2-3   garlic cloves

Using cheesecloth, make a bundle of the peppercorns, bay leaf, chili flake, allspice, and garlic. Tie off the bundle with butcher's twine, leaving a length of twine free. Slice the onions into halves, then slice the halves into ¼ inch strips.

Bring the water, sugar, spice bundle, and vinegar to a simmer, stirring to dissolve the sugar. Place cut onions in a container, leaving space at the top. Pour warm brine over the onions, making sure the onions are completely covered. Add the spice bundle to the container. Cover the top of the container with plastic wrap, pressing down to the surface of the brine so that the onions are completely submerged. Let sit in the fridge for a few days until the onions reach their desired taste.

LEMONGRASS ROCKFISH

7 lemongrass stocks, whiter parts, peeled, sliced thin, and chopped fine

12 garlic cloves, chopped fine

1 shallot, chopped fine

8 kaffir lime leaves, sliced very thin, then chopped fine

2 3-inch pieces of ginger, peeled, sliced thin, and minced

3 jalapeños, seeded and chopped

1 orange, zest chopped fine and the juice of same orange

3 Tbl fish sauce

24 oz rockfish fillet, skinless, boneless, cut into 6 oz. portions (ask your fish monger to cut out the rib bones)

- kosher salt

- white pepper, ground

MARINADE: Whisk first eight ingredients together well in a stainless steel mixing bowl. Pour over portion sized fish and let marinate for 3 hours prior to cooking. Lemongrass marinade for fish yields 1½ quarts.

COOK FISH: Preheat oven to 350°F. Remove fish fillets from the marinade and place on a lightly oiled, heavy sheet pan. Season fish fillets with kosher salt and ground white pepper. Top each fillet with the Gremolata (recipe below) and pat down gently to make a ⅓-inch crust. Bake fish in a convection oven for approximately 15 minutes. Time will vary depending on the thickness of the fish. The crust should be browned nicely and the fish should not resist a paring knife gently pushed into the thickest part. Cook the fish to an internal temperature of 145°F.

TO SERVE: Place fish on a plate with the browned crust up and accompany it with tri- color quinoa or farro. Sautéed greens or seasonal vegetables would complete the plate.

GREMOLATA: A mixture of panko bread crumbs moistened with melted butter, seasoned with Kaffir lime leaf (finely chopped), orange zest, finely chopped garlic, and chopped parsley.

SESAME & MINT ABALONE SALAD

½ lb shelled abalone steaks

1 medium cucumber (or 2-3 Persian cucumbers)

4 lemons, juiced

2 Tbl rice wine vinegar

1 Tbl sugar

4 red radishes

½ bunch mint leaves, chopped into chiffonade strips

1 tsp sesame seeds

1 cup white wine

1 tsp chopped garlic

- salt

Pound raw abalone steaks until flat. Heat wine, garlic, and ¼ cup lemon juice to a simmering boil. Poach abalone steaks in the wine solution until barely cooked through, about 40 seconds. Immediately shock the abalone in ice water to stop the cooking process. Remove from ice water and pat dry. Cut the abalone steaks into thin strips.

Shave radishes and cucumber (lengthwise) and then cut into thin strips, similar in size to the abalone. Marinate the abalone, cucumber, and radish in the sugar, salt, and vinegar with 4 tablespoons lemon juice. Garnish the marinated salad with sesame seeds and mint. Serve.

BUTTERNUT SQUASH SOUP

with maple whipped cream

This is a great vegetarian soup! You can omit the maple whipped cream to make it completely vegan.

1 large or 2 medium sized butternut squash

- sunflower or canola oil
- salt and white pepper

1 cup heavy whipping cream
1 Tbl real maple syrup

BUTTERNUT SQUASH SOUP: Preheat oven to 425°F. Cut squash in half lengthwise and scoop out seeds. Place cut side up on an oiled sheet tray. Drizzle squash halves liberally with oil and season with salt and white pepper. Flip halves over so that the skin side is now facing up. Roast until flesh is tender. You should be able to stick a knife through the skin and into the flesh without resistance: approximately 15-20 minutes.

Let the squash cool slightly. Scoop out cooked flesh into a blender or food processor. Puree the butternut flesh until smooth, adding water as needed to reach your desired soup consistency. Adjust seasoning with salt and white pepper as needed.

MAPLE WHIPPED CREAM: Whisk heavy cream with maple syrup to taste until the cream has thickened to medium-firm peaks.

BUTTERMILK BORSCHT SOUP

with jasmine flower

Serves 5 cups

1 lb   red beets, trimmed and cleaned

1   small red onion, peeled and cut into quarters

2   medium carrots, cut into 1 inch pieces

1   celery rib, cut into 1 inch pieces

1   clove garlic, smashed and peeled

1 Tbl   olive oil

-   kosher salt

1   sprig thyme

1   jasmine tea flower bud

3 cups   vegetable broth

-   white pepper, freshly ground

½ cup   light buttermilk

1½ Tbl   chopped fresh dill

-   sour cream or crème fraiche to garnish

Take two large sheets of heavy duty foil and lay them on top of each other on the worktable. Put the vegetables and garlic in the center of the foil, drizzle with olive oil, season with ½ teaspoon salt, and add the thyme and jasmine tea bud wrapped in a piece of cheesecloth tied with a string. Seal the foil to make a tight package. Put the package in a roasting pan. Roast until the beets can be pierced easily with a knife, about 1 to 1½ hours at 425°F. When the beets are cool enough to handle, peel them – the skins should slide right off with a bit of pressure from your fingers.

Remove the jasmine tea ball and put ½ of the vegetables in a food processor with ½ of the broth, and puree. A high speed blender could also be used to make a smoother soup. Transfer the puree to a saucepan. Repeat with the remaining vegetables and broth. Stir in kosher salt and white pepper to taste and simmer over medium heat until the flavors come together, about 10 minutes. Remove from the heat and stir in the buttermilk. Strain as you wish to obtain the desired consistency. Re-blend with high speed blender to make it ultra smooth.

Ladle borscht into bowls and garnish with sour cream and dill.

STAR ANISE PASTRY CREAM

1 cup	whole milk
½	vanilla bean, halved and scraped
4	large egg yolks
5-6	star anise seeds
½ cup	sugar
2 Tbl	cornstarch
2 Tbl	butter

Mix the milk with vanilla and star anise in a medium saucepan. (It's okay to include the empty vanilla bean shell in the cream along with the scrapings.) Very slowly bring the milk up to scalding, giving the star anise and vanilla time to steep and infuse flavor to the milk. Strain out the star anise seeds and empty vanilla bean shell. Whisk together egg yolks, sugar, and cornstarch until well combined and smooth. Slowly add the heated milk into the egg mixture little by little, whisking constantly. Return mixture to pot and return to medium heat, still whisking. Cook until mixture thickens, about 3 minutes. (It is easier to switch to a wooden spoon or rubber spatula for this part, as a whisk can make the mixture too frothy.)

Once thickened, remove from heat, add butter and continue to stir for an additional minute. Pour mixture through a fine mesh strainer into a chilled bowl. Cover the bowl with plastic wrap and press the plastic to meet the surface of the mixture. This prevents the cream from forming a "skin" as it cools. Chill pastry cream until set, anywhere from 2 to 24 hours.

PORT POACHED PEARS

6 cups	port wine
2½ cups	organic cane sugar
2	large oranges, zest and juice
2 Tbl	chopped fresh ginger
1	3-inch cinnamon stick
8	medium-firm, ripe pears, peeled and cored
¾ tsp	cornstarch
¼ cup	fresh orange juice

In a large, wide, non-reactive saucepan, combine the port, sugar, zest, and juice of the oranges, ginger, and cinnamon stick and bring to a boil. Lower the heat and simmer for 4 minutes. Add the pears and return to the simmer. Gently simmer until the pears are cooked through and tender, testing the pears with a toothpick. The cooking time will vary greatly depending on the type and size of pear used. When tender, remove from the heat. Strain 1 cup of the poaching liquid into a small saucepan. Leave the pears in their liquid while making the sauce.

Dissolve the cornstarch in the orange juice and add to the small saucepan containing the cup of poaching liquid. Bring to a simmer and cook for 2 minutes until lightly thickened. Remove from the heat and set aside to cool.

Serve the pears sliced and fanned in shallow bowls or on plates. Spoon some of the sauce over and around the slices. Garnish with 2 or 3 orange segments, mint sprigs, and whipped cream or ice cream.

NOTE: These pears can be poached several days ahead of time and be kept in the poaching liquid. These pears are very versatile and can be used for salad, for duck or chicken entrées, or as we used here, for dessert.